Student Book

New International Edition

Grade 5

Tara Lievesley, Deborah Herridge
Series editor: John Stringer

ALWAYS LEARNING

PEARSON

Pearson Education Limited is a company incorporated in England and Wales having its registered office at Edinburgh Gate, Harlow, Essex, CM20 2JE.

Registered company number: 872828

www.pearsonglobalschools.com

Text © Pearson Education Limited 2012
First published 2003. This edition published 2012.

20 19 18 17 16
IMP 10 9 8 7 6 5

British Library Cataloguing in Publication Data
A catalogue record for this book is available from the British Library

ISBN 978 0 435 13359 7

Edited by Glenys Davis
Designed by TechSet Limited
Original illustrations © Pearson Education Limited, 2003, 2009, 2012
Illustrated by Rosie Brooks, Beehive Illustration Ltd
Picture research by Louise Edgeworth
Cover images: Front: Alamy Images
Indexed by Indexing Specialists (UK) Ltd
Printed and bound in Malaysia, CTP-PJB

Acknowledgements
The publisher would like to thank the following for their kind permission to reproduce their photographs:

(Key: b-bottom; c-centre; l-left; r-right; t-top)

Alamy Images: 7tr, 14bl, 16cl, 19br, 23cr, 26tr, 29l, 29r, 29bl, 29br, 36cl, 39c, 49l; Corbis: 56bl, 64br; DK Images: 26tl; Fotolia.com: 1cr, 6tr, 6cl, 11bl, 17tl, 24tr, 28bl, 62bl, 73bl, 75tr; Getty Images: 34br, 51cr; Glow Images: 12br, 58bl; Pearson Education Ltd: Trevor Clifford 24bl; Science Photo Library Ltd: 2tr, 6bc, 13tl, 20tr, 20cr, 38tr, 68bl, 69tl, 76bl; Shutterstock.com: 10tr, 12tl, 17bl, 20bl, 25br, 27tr, 28tr, 28br, 38bl, 48cl, 53tr, 53br, 59tr, 59cl, 63tl, 66tr, 66br, 74tr, 74bl, 76tr

All other images © Pearson Education

Every effort has been made to trace the copyright holders and we apologise in advance for any unintentional omissions. We would be pleased to insert the appropriate acknowledgement in any subsequent edition of this publication.

Contents

How to use this book

At the beginning of each Unit are lists of things you should already know and should be able to do.

This shows words in the Unit that are important. Learn and use these in your work.

This box tells you what the lesson is about.

Find out what coloured words in bold mean in the Glossary at the back of the book.

Think about these questions. By the end of the Unit you will know how to answer them.

Try these activities. Your teacher will help you.

These boxes give you some fascinating facts.

Unit 1: Microbes

Do you like yoghurt? Did you know it is made from sour milk. 'Bugs' called **micro-organisms** or microbes make it turn sour. Microbes are so small we can't see them without a microscope, but for such small creatures they are very important. Helpful microbes make cheese, wine and bread. Some microbes can be harmful, and make foods bad for us to eat. Helpful or harmful, we can't live without them. They are even inside you, helping you digest your food!

What do you know?
- All living things feed, grow and reproduce.
- All living things need nutrients to be healthy.
- All living things have a **life cycle** to ensure survival.
- Different organisms are found in different habitats.

Skills check
Can you...
- measure volume and temperature?
- make careful observations?
- explain what you find out using your science knowledge?

Words to learn
bacteria
micro-organism
germ
microbe
mould
pasteurize
sterilize
virus
yeast

Let's find out...
Do you eat 'fresh food'? You may think you do, but is it really fresh? Look at the photo. Which of these items are really fresh? Which are **preserved**? Can you explain why some food is preserved?

Unit 1: Microbes 1

Using microbes

Things to learn
- How microbes can be used to make food and drink.
- How microbes can cause us to be ill.
- Whether we can also use microbes to make us well.

Edible mould
Mould is a microbe. Would you eat mouldy bread? No. But people eat blue cheese. The blue 'veins' in cheese are also mould! The cheese has been made so only the right type of mould grows in it. This makes it safe and tasty to eat.

Meat can have microbes growing on it. It starts to smell when the microbes are growing. If you eat food that smells like this, it will give you food poisoning. Your body will throw the bad food out of you. You will be very sick.

If food is not **preserved**, microbes feed from it before we do. In what ways do we preserve food?

How can we package food to prevent microbes spoiling it? Think about drying, canning, cooking and freezing.

Cheese with microbes growing on it

A close-up of microbes

Microbe wars
If you have an infection, the doctor may give you an antibiotic. This kills the microbe making you ill. The antibiotic may have been made by another microbe! You must take all of the antibiotic or the microbes will change to fight it. We also use microbes to make other chemicals to improve our lives. This is called '**biotechnology**'.

Things to do

How yeast rises
Yeast is a microbe used to make food and drink, like ginger beer and bread. When it is growing, it produces a gas called carbon dioxide. This can be seen as bubbles in drinks. It makes bread rise. You can see the holes in bread made by gas bubbles. But what conditions produce most gas? How can you measure the gas?

Put some warm water in a glass bottle. Add some yeast, and some sugar to feed it. Stretch a balloon over the top of the bottle. What happens to the balloon? Can you explain why?

- Now try using cold water. What differences do you predict? Try it and see.
- Is there a 'best' temperature to make yeast grow well?

Alexander Fleming was an important scientist in the last century

Dig deeper
Find out:
- what important discovery Alexander Fleming made
- more about how the discovery was made.

I wonder...
Canning kills microbes by heating and driving off air, so the microbes have no oxygen. What do freezing and drying do to microbes? How do salting, **curing** and **irradiating** work?

Did you know?
- The biotechnology industry is growing. It will change our lives completely by the end of this century, just as computers did last century.
- Salting, canning, drying, irradiating, **boiling**, curing and freezing are all methods of preserving foods.

6 Heinemann Explore Science Grade 5

Unit 1: Microbes 7

This box tells you what you will find out during the lesson. Your teacher will help you.

Use what you have learned to answer these questions.

Here you find answers to important questions.

Check what you have learned.

Investigating microbes

Your challenge
- Discover the conditions microbes require to grow well.
- Decide the best way to observe the microbes' growth.
- Explain whether the evidence shows that microbes are living things.

We will use food to grow the microbes. We will put food into different plastic bags in the same place.

We want to use the same type of food in different conditions. This will be dry bread and wet bread in warm and cold conditions.

What to check
- Class 5J have agreed to count the microbe colonies produced after four days. Which bread will produce the most mould? What do they need to keep the same?
- Now try it yourselves. What do you think will happen?
- Will the light in the fridge make a difference to the results?

What to do
Class 5J want to investigate microbes. How will they grow them? What will they observe? Would you use their idea, or one of your own?

I wonder why the fridge light only stays on a short while?

I feel like feeding, growing and dividing when it gets warm.

What you need
- some bread
- transparent plastic bags or containers
- ties for the bags

Have you noticed the air warms up when the light comes on?

What we need is to find somewhere warm and damp.

What did you find?

Class 5J produced this table of results from their investigation:

Conditions	What grew and why
warm and damp	25
warm and dry	10
cold and damp	14
cold and dry	1

Class 5J can only draw a bar chart of their results. Why?
- Draw a graph of your results. What pattern can you see? Which conditions does this microbe grow best in? What did you notice about the bread with the most colonies on it?
- Is a microbe a living thing? What evidence in your investigation supports this?

You must NOT open the plastic bags once they are sealed with the flies. Microbes can be harmful and their spores can travel through the air.

Can you do better?
Class 5J only had one set of results. This doesn't make the results very reliable. What could you do to ensure that you had really reliable evidence?

Now predict
- Class 5A are also investigating microbes growing on food. They are trying to prevent their food from producing mould. What conditions would keep their food longer?
- Write an instruction label for the food, to show how to keep the food fresh.

Unit 1: Review

What have you learned?
- Microbes can cause illness.
- They can also cause useful changes and harmful decay.
- Microbes can be used to make foods like yoghurt and bread.
- Microbes are living things and need warm and damp conditions to grow well.
- Food poisoning is caused by microbes.
- Microbes can be transferred from person to person.

Find out more about...
- how microbes make other foods.
- the immune system and how to fight disease.

Check-up
Class 3M about to eat their lunch. They have just been doing some work outside and haven't washed their hands. Explain to them why they should wash their hands before eating their lunch.

The answer!
Remember the question about food?
If food is left out, microbes will be able to grow on it, perhaps making the food harmful to eat. However, food preservation changes the condition of food to prevent microbes growing on it. Jam is preserved by boiling sugar and sealing the sugar and fruit in an airtight jar. Milk is pasteurized at a very high temperature.

Unit 1: Microbes

Do you like yoghurt? Did you know it is made from sour milk? 'Bugs' called **micro-organisms** or microbes make it turn sour. Microbes are so small we can't see them without a microscope, but for such small creatures they are very important. Helpful microbes make cheese, wine and bread. Some microbes can be harmful, and make foods bad for us to eat. Helpful or harmful, we can't live without them. They are even inside you, helping you digest your food!

What do you know?

- All living things feed, grow and reproduce.
- All living things need nutrients to be healthy.
- All living things have a **life cycle** to ensure survival.
- Different organisms are found in different habitats.

Skills check

Can you...

- measure volume and temperature?
- make careful observations?
- explain what you find out using your science knowledge?

Words to learn

bacteria
micro-organism
germ
microbe
mould

pasteurize
sterilize
virus
yeast

Let's find out...

Do you eat 'fresh food'? You may think you do, but is it really fresh? Look at the photo. Which of these items are really fresh? Which are **preserved**? Can you explain why some food is preserved?

Microbes and you

Things to learn
- How big microbes are.
- Whether some microbes can be harmful.
- How microbes help us survive.

This microbe causes yellow fever

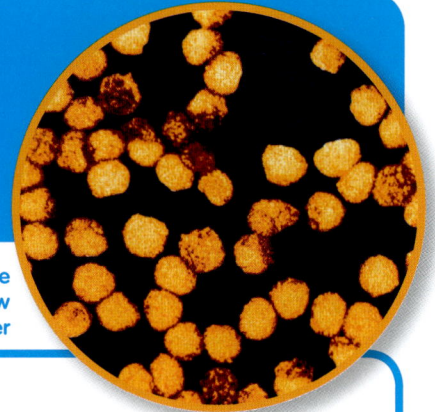

Invisible life

Microbes are too small to see with our eyes. Ten of them might fit in the millimetre measure of a ruler. Many of them are much smaller. So how do we know they exist?

When you see mouldy food, you are seeing colonies or groups of microbes. Yoghurt and cheese are made using microbes growing in the food.

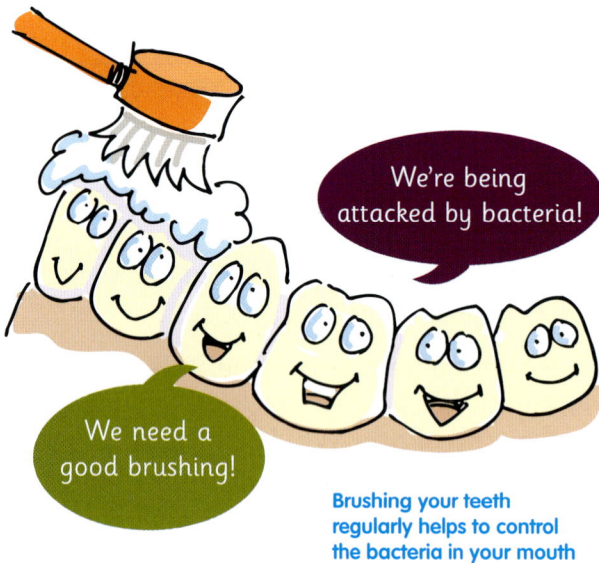

We're being attacked by bacteria!

We need a good brushing!

Brushing your teeth regularly helps to control the bacteria in your mouth

Attack!

Your mouth is under attack all the time from **bacteria**. These bacteria are a type of microbe. They grow really well in the conditions in your mouth. The bacteria turn the **sugar** from our food into acid. The acid attacks our teeth, causing tooth decay. Regular brushing reduces the number of bacteria.

When you are ill you react to the microbes that are attacking your body. Chicken pox and some kinds of colds and flu are caused by microbes.

Athlete's foot is caused by microbes. They are a kind of **mould**, or fungus, related to mushrooms!

How do these diseases spread between people? What does the rhyme 'coughs and sneezes spread diseases' mean?

Things to do

Making compost

If there weren't microbes to break down and rot dead animal and plant material, we would be knee-deep in waste. There would be no way of replacing nutrients in the soil that the plants need to grow and be healthy. There wouldn't be any **compost** to put on the garden either.

What rots to form compost? Collect a variety of objects and see if they decay. Put them outside somewhere safe. Leave your collection of objects for a couple of weeks. Then look at them. Which ones have rotted most? Remember not to handle the rotted material!

I wonder...

If the word 'bacteria' is the plural, then what is the word for a single microbe of this kind?

Dig deeper

Find out:

- more about the largest waste management plant in the world, based in Qatar
- more about how microbes were first discovered and who discovered them
- which microbes they discovered.

Did you know?

- 500 bacteria could fit on a full stop!
- You would need 160 billion bacteria to fill a teaspoon!
- Some bacteria can make stone decay. They produce acid, just like the bacteria in our mouths. The acid is so strong it dissolves the stone away.

Investigating microbes

Your challenge

- Discover the conditions microbes require to grow well.
- Decide the best way to observe the microbes' growth.
- Explain whether the evidence shows that microbes are living things.

We will use food to grow the microbes. We will put food into different plastic bags in the same place.

We want to use the same type of food in different conditions. This will be dry bread and wet bread in warm and cold conditions.

What to check

- Class 5J have agreed to count the microbe colonies produced after four days. Which bread will produce the most mould? What do they need to keep the same?
- Now try it yourselves. What do you think will happen?
- Will the light in the fridge make a difference to the results?

What to do

Class 5J want to investigate microbes. How will they grow them? What will they observe? Would you use their idea, or one of your own?

I wonder why the fridge light only stays on a short while?

I feel like feeding, growing and dividing when it gets warm.

What you need

- some bread
- transparent plastic bags or containers
- ties for the bags

Have you noticed the air warms up when the light comes on?

What we need is to find somewhere warm and damp.

What did you find?

Class 5J produced this table of results from their investigation:

Conditions	What grew and why
warm and damp	25
warm and dry	10
cold and damp	14
cold and dry	1

Class 5J can only draw a bar chart of their results. Why?

- Draw a graph of your results. What pattern can you see? Which conditions does this microbe grow best in? What did you notice about the bread with the most colonies on it?
- Is a microbe a living thing? What evidence in your investigation supports this?

Can you do better?

Class 5J only had one set of results. This doesn't make the results very reliable. What could you do to ensure that you had really reliable evidence?

You must NOT open the plastic bags once they are sealed with the ties. Microbes can be harmful and their spores can travel through the air.

Now predict

- Class 5A are also investigating microbes growing on food. They are trying to prevent their food from producing mould. What conditions would keep their food longer?
- Write an instruction label for the food, to show how to keep the food fresh.

Things to learn

- How microbes can be used to make food and drink.
- How microbes can cause us to be ill.
- Whether we can also use microbes to make us well.

Edible mould

Mould is a microbe. Would you eat mouldy bread? No. But people eat blue cheese. The blue 'veins' in cheese are also mould! The cheese has been made so only the right type of mould grows in it. This makes it safe and tasty to eat.

Meat can have microbes growing on it. It starts to smell when the microbes are growing. If you eat food that smells like this, it will give you food poisoning. Your body will throw the bad food out of you. You will be very sick.

Cheese with microbes growing on it

If food is not **preserved**, microbes feed from it before we do. In what ways do we preserve food?

How can we package food to prevent microbes spoiling it? Think about drying, canning, cooking and freezing.

A close-up of microbes

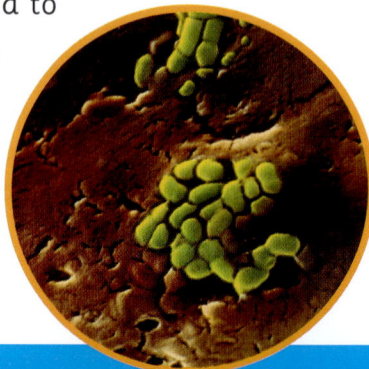

Microbe wars

If you have an infection, the doctor may give you an antibiotic. This kills the microbe making you ill. The antibiotic may have been made by another microbe! You must take all of the antibiotic or the microbes will change to fight it. We also use microbes to make other chemicals to improve our lives. This is called '**biotechnology**'.

Things to do

How yeast rises

Yeast is a microbe used to make food and drink, like ginger beer and bread. When it is growing, it produces a gas called carbon dioxide. This can be seen as bubbles in drinks. It makes bread rise. You can see the holes in bread made by gas bubbles. But what conditions produce most gas? How can you measure the gas?

Put some warm water in a glass bottle. Add some yeast, and some sugar to feed it. Stretch a balloon over the top of the bottle. What happens to the balloon? Can you explain why?

- Now try using cold water. What differences do you predict? Try it and see.
- Is there a 'best' temperature to make yeast grow well?

I wonder...

Canning kills microbes by heating and driving off air, so the microbes have no oxygen. What do freezing and drying do to microbes? How do salting, **curing** and **irradiating** work?

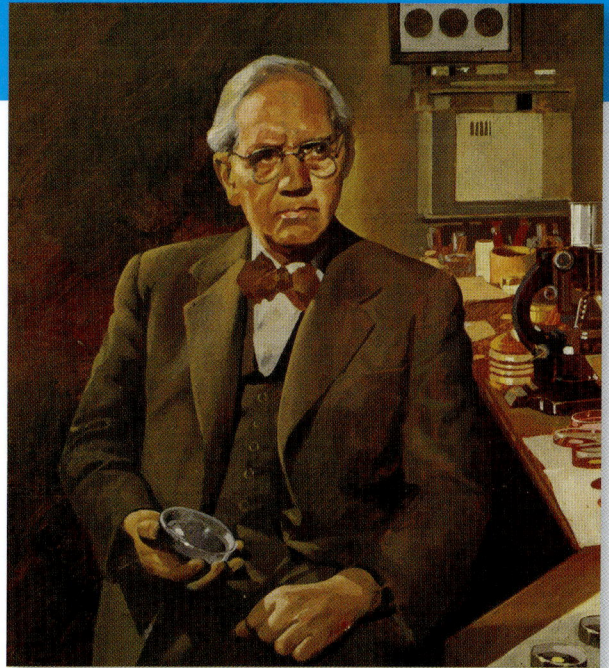

Alexander Fleming was an important scientist in the last century

Dig deeper

Find out:
- what important discovery Alexander Fleming made
- more about how the discovery was made.

Did you know?

- The biotechnology industry is growing. It will change our lives completely by the end of this century, just as computers did last century.
- Salting, canning, drying, irradiating, **boiling**, curing and freezing are all methods of preserving foods.

What have you learned?
- Microbes can cause illness.
- They can also cause useful changes and harmful decay.
- Microbes can be used to make foods like yoghurt and bread.
- Microbes are living things and need warm and damp conditions to grow well.
- Food poisoning is caused by microbes.
- Microbes can be transferred from person to person.

Find out more about...
- how microbes make other foods.
- the immune system and how to fight disease.

Check-up

Class 3M are about to eat their lunch. They have just been doing some work outside and haven't washed their hands. Explain to them why they should wash their hands before eating their lunch.

The answer!

Remember the question about food?

If food is left out, microbes will be able to grow on it, perhaps making the food harmful to eat. However, food preservation changes the condition of food to prevent microbes growing on it. Jam is preserved by boiling sugar and sealing the sugar and fruit in an airtight jar. Milk is **pasteurized** at a very high temperature.

Unit 2: Keeping healthy

Why aren't you allowed fries for dinner every day? What exactly is a 'couch potato'? It's no good just eating foods that look nice! We have to eat the right sorts of foods or we become ill. Food helps keep us healthy. We need to exercise as well. This helps us stay fit.

Skills check

Can you...

- compare observations that you make?
- decide what to investigate and collect the evidence?
- use a stopwatch to time?
- count carefully?

What do you know?

- The names of some parts of your body.
- Which foods are good for growth and which are good for warmth.
- That we need to eat, to grow and be healthy.
- A balanced diet is important for health.

Let's find out...

If an adult was lazy, overweight and smoked, why might their doctor worry about their health? What might the doctor suggest they do? What kind of food would the doctor suggest they eat? What other things might they do to get their health back?

Things to learn

- What kind of diet we need to eat to stay healthy.
- What else we need to stay healthy.
- How our muscles work when we exercise.

Chocolate ice cream and fries

Would you like chocolate ice cream and fries for dinner? Would you like it every day? After a couple of days you might want something different.

Eating different things makes food interesting. It helps make sure you have a **balanced diet**. Can you remember the food groups you need to eat?

How much energy do you need?

Some foods are essential to keep us healthy. Some help us grow. Others give us energy. **Starch** and **sugar** are **carbohydrates**. This type of food gives us energy. The energy is measured in kilocalories or kilojoules. A child your age needs about 2400 kilocalories each day. Even asleep you are still using energy. What are you using it for? Why do you need more than an adult?

An athlete needs more energy than the average adult. Why? Think what an athlete does.

Things to do

Apples, oranges, peas, carrots and peppers!

Every day you should eat five portions of fresh fruit and vegetables. This doesn't always mean potatoes and cabbage! You can eat oranges, apples, peas and carrots. Why do we need fresh fruit and vegetables every day?

- Make a list of the fruit and vegetables you usually eat. Over the next week, every time you eat one, tick it.
- Make a chart to show which fruit and vegetables you eat most.

There are many kinds of fruit and vegetables to choose from

I wonder...

Why would an athlete eat lots of rice, pasta, fresh fruit and vegetables? What do these foods provide?

Dig deeper

Find out:
- what makes celery interesting
- what else we need to do to be fit and healthy.

Did you know?

- Your digestive system starts working even before you eat your food. The sight and smell makes your mouth water!
- You are very strong. If all your muscles were one big muscle, it could lift a bus!

Your heart

Things to learn

- How our heart is protected.
- What our hearts do.

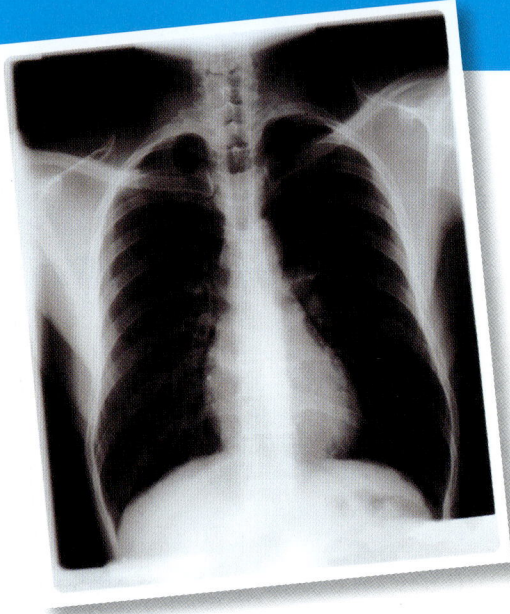

An X-ray image of your chest and ribcage

Crash hats and ribcages

When you ride a bicycle you probably wear a helmet. This protects an essential part of your body. Without your brain nothing else will work.

Your ribs make a protective cage around your heart and lungs. Soldiers used to wear armoured breastplates to protect their chests from injury.

A stethoscope carries the sound of your heart straight to the doctor's ears

What sound does your heart make?

Place your hand where you think your heart is. What can you feel? Put the palms of your hands over your ears and try to block out any noise. You will hear your pulse. How does it sound?

Doctors use a stethoscope to listen to your heart. It cuts out all sounds except the beating of your heart. They listen to check if it is working properly. They understand how well the heart is working. Doctors also use an electronic heart monitor.

This is a heart valve made of plastic

Find out:
- about the heart and how it pumps blood
- what valves do and how they prevent blood flowing in the wrong direction.

Things to do

Your very own pump

Your heart is a large muscle. It has two sides. The left side is bigger than the right. This side pumps blood round your body. The right side pumps it only to your lungs.

- Use a washing-up bottle filled with water. Find out how hard the heart pumps to get blood around your body. Measure how far the water goes into the air. Your heart would pump water about 30 m up!

Did you know?

- The average human heart weighs only 280 g. It is the same size as your fist.
- Your heart is in the middle of your chest. But it is larger on the left than it is on the right.
- Your left lung is slightly smaller than the right. This makes room for your heart.
- The smaller you are, the faster your heart is likely to beat.

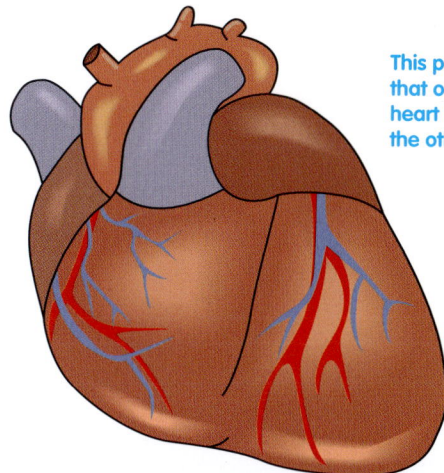

This picture shows that one side of the heart is larger than the other

I wonder...

Your **pulse** is a pressure wave from your heartbeat. You can feel your pulse in many places. Where can you find it?

Pumping blood

Things to learn

- How blood gets carried around the body.
- The three types of blood vessels and their roles.
- What blood carries around our body.

fine capillary

thin-walled vein

thick-walled artery

Three for one

Three types of **vessel** or tube carry blood in your body – **arteries**, **capillaries** and **veins**. Arteries have thick elastic walls. They carry blood away from our heart. Capillaries are very small tubes that join arteries and veins. Veins have thinner walls than arteries, but are bigger than capillaries. They carry blood back to the heart.

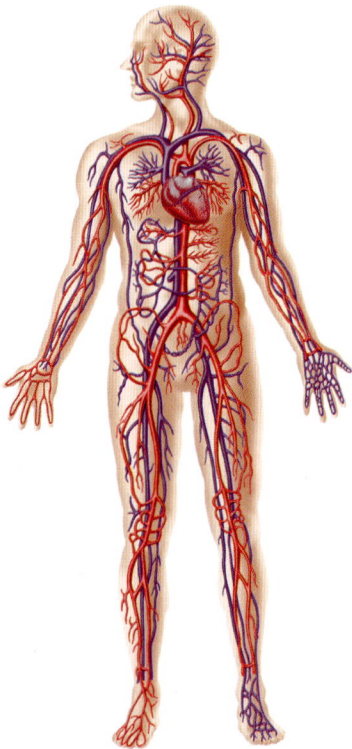

A network of vessels carries blood all around your body

Blood's journey

'Hi! I'm your blood. I have to pick up oxygen from the lungs and take it to the rest of the body in the arteries. I have to call at the brain, the lungs and even the heart!

'Next stop is the liver. These tubes are getting smaller. The artery is turning into a capillary. I have to deliver some oxygen here. Further up the capillary now. It's getting wider! Nearly into a vein. Just need to stop at the kidneys so I can be cleaned, then back to the heart.

'I go from your heart to every organ in your body.'

Things to do

How does it work?

Look at this picture of the heart. It has four chambers. There are four tubes or vessels coming in or out of the chambers. Which ones do you think carry blood into the heart? Look at the muscles on both sides of the heart. Which side pumps the blood around the body? What does the other side do?

- Find out the names for the chambers and vessels in the heart.

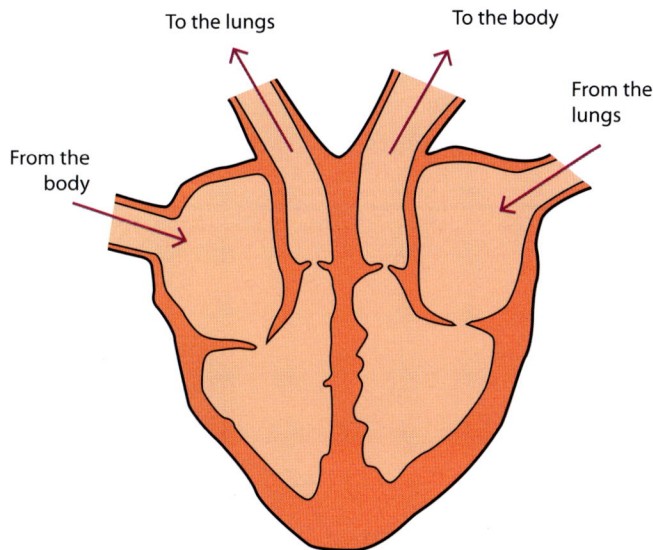

To the lungs

To the body

From the lungs

From the body

I wonder…

Can you make your heart beat faster by thinking about it? What makes your heart beat fast or slow?

Dig deeper

Find out:
- how each part of your heart works
- why your heart beats faster when you exercise
- what blood is made of.

Did you know?

- Your heart beats about 3000 million times during your lifetime.
- Your blood travels through about 96 000 km of blood vessels. This is a quarter of the way to the Moon!
- There are five billion red blood cells in every litre of your blood. They carry the oxygen round your body.

Things to learn

- How we can measure our heart rate.
- How our pulse and heartbeat are related.

Faster, faster

When we exercise, our heart beats faster. It has to pump blood faster around our body. Why does it have to do this? What does our blood carry to our muscles?

As well as other things, blood carries oxygen. Our muscles need oxygen to be active. If our muscles move faster, they need more oxygen. Our heart has to pump faster to deliver the oxygen. But will our heart just keep on beating faster and faster? Or will it slow down again? When?

Give it a rest

Your heart beats continuously throughout your lifetime. It will beat about 100 000 times in one day. It beats for about 70 or more years without a break. How many times will it beat in one week? Or in a year? It never stops. Or does it?

Your heart takes a break between every beat! If you live for 70 years, then your heart is actually resting for about 40 years!

PUMP ROOM

I wonder…

Is there a pattern between the number of heartbeats per minute and the size of the animal?

Things to do

How fast is yours?

Your heart beats at least 70 times each minute. You don't need to feel your heart to count how fast it beats. You can feel your pulse instead. Your pulse is the wave of blood flowing through your arteries from your heart. You can feel the 'push' of your heart.

- Place your fingers on your wrist to feel your pulse. Sit down and count the beats for one minute. Record the number. Do it again. Is the number exactly the same?

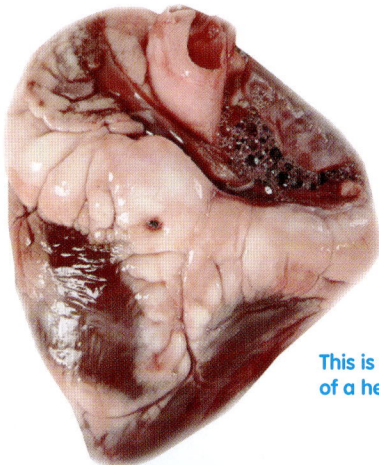

This is a picture of a heart

Dig deeper

Find out:
- about your blood pressure.

Did you know?

- Your heart uses 7 per cent of all the oxygen used by the body. Your brain uses 25 per cent.
- The human heart beats about 70 times a minute when resting. A hummingbird's beats 1300 times each minute. A blue whale's beats ten times a minute!

Investigating pulse rate

Your challenge

- Find out what affects your pulse rate.
- Decide what measurements to take.
- Present and explain the results.

So blood takes oxygen to the muscles.

Yes, and when we exercise we need more oxygen. So our heart beats faster.

I wonder which exercise makes your heart beat fastest?

What to do

Class 5E want to see if their predictions about exercise are correct. They have different ideas about what to do. They have decided how to record their evidence. They will count their pulse rates for one minute and put the results in a table.

We will take our pulse rate at rest and after each exercise.

You could take your pulse after each type of exercise.

We will take our pulse rate three times at rest, then three times after each activity.

What you need

- stopwatches

What to check

- Where will you measure your pulse?
- How many people will do the exercise?
- What will you keep the same to make it a fair test?

We will do the same exercise for one minute, two minutes and three minutes.

We can then take the pulse rate three times after each period of exercise.

What did you find?

Class 5E decided to change the type of exercise. To get more reliable results, they took their pulse three times for one minute. They made an average of the results. They recorded in bpm (beats per minute).

Type of exercise	Pulse rate (bpm)
sitting	70
jogging	95
running	130
sit-ups	105
skipping	124

- What kind of chart can you produce using Class 5E's results? Draw a chart on the computer. How many different types of chart can you draw?
- What does your chart show? Which exercise gave the highest pulse rate? Why do you think this exercise was the hardest? Was your prediction correct?

Dig deeper

What practical problems did you have with the investigation? Think about timing and the person doing the exercise.

Now predict

- Class 5A are going to run a relay race. They want to know what will happen to their heart as they run. Draw a sketch graph to show what you think will happen to each student as they start running, while they run and after they hand over the baton. Give reasons for your graph shape.
- Class 5G are going to do the same investigation as Class 5E. They are only going to take each pulse once. Explain why they should take the pulse at least twice. How else can they make their results more reliable?

Drugs and you

Things to learn

● Why tobacco is not good for us.
● How tobacco and other drugs can affect our bodies.
● The difference between medicines and drugs.

All change

A **drug** is a substance that causes our bodies to change. A drug can change the way you feel. It may make your heart beat faster. It may affect your thinking and make you slow to react. Some drugs are **addictive**. Once you start using them, you find it very hard to stop. **Medicines** are also drugs, but they are used only to prevent or treat illnesses and injuries.

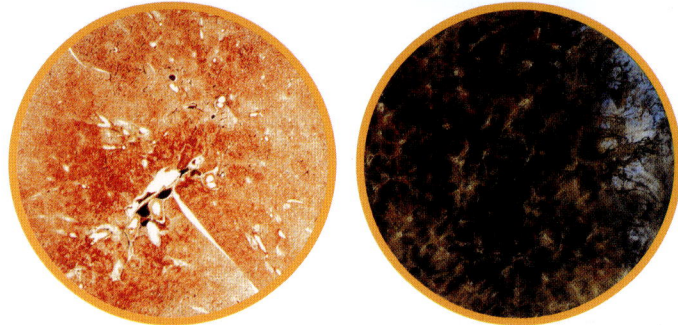

Compare the tissue in the healthy lung on the left with the one affected by smoke on the right

Nicotine

Smoking tobacco, like cigarettes, is addictive. The addictive drug is called nicotine. The nicotine doesn't make us ill. It is the tobacco smoke that is unhealthy. The smoke contains tar.

These medicines are all drugs – but not all drugs are medicines

Not looking so good

Smokers may have dull, lined skin. Tobacco stains your teeth, nails and makes your fingers yellow. It can give you bad breath. Women who smoke may have thin legs and wrinkled skin. Pregnant mothers who smoke can harm their unborn baby.

Things to do

Don't quit, just don't start

Lots of people try to give up smoking. It is better to not start at all. Doctors can use information about illnesses caused by smoking to show how bad it is for you.

Dr Quitit has to give a presentation to help some smokers stop smoking. He is short of time and needs your help. Can you find out more about smoking, take some notes and make the presentation for him?

Dig deeper

Find out:
- what an addiction is
- the sort of things you can be addicted to.

I wonder...

Why do medicine bottles have child-proof caps?

Did you know?

- Coffee is a stimulant which contains caffeine. Caffeine keeps you awake.
- Tobacco smoke contains carbon monoxide. This is a poisonous gas. It takes the place of oxygen in your blood so that your heart and lungs have to work harder.
- Just being near to smokers might mean you become ill. This is called passive smoking.

What have you learned?

- Our hearts are protected by our ribs and pump blood around our body.
- There are three types of blood vessels.
- Our blood carries oxygen around our body in blood vessels.
- When we exercise our heart beats faster and our pulse rate get faster.
- Nicotine is a drug in tobacco that can affect our bodies.
- Some drugs are medicines. Some are harmful.

Find out more about…

- how to keep your heart healthy
- how William Harvey discovered how the heart works.

Check-up

Class 5G have been running a cross-country race. They feel hot and tired. They are breathing heavily. They can hear the blood rushing in their ears.

- Explain why they are breathing heavily and can hear their blood.
- Explain what their hearts are doing and why they are beating differently.
- Explain what will happen when they stop running.

The answer!

Do you remember the question about the unhealthy adult? The doctor would ask them to eat plenty of fresh fruit and vegetables every day. The doctor might suggest giving up fatty foods. They might also suggest taking gentle exercise and building it up slowly. The heart has to get used to pumping blood around the body faster. Exercise would use up stored fat. The doctor would encourage them to give up smoking. This would make the lungs work better and the person could exercise without getting short of breath.

Unit 3: Life cycles

Animals and plants change as they get older. How they change may differ. They both produce new versions of themselves. They both spread from place to place, but in different ways. How do they do this? How are they similar? Or different?

What do you know?

- Animals need food to grow and be healthy.
- Plants need light and water to grow well.
- Plants have stems, roots and leaves.
- Our skeletons grow bigger as we grow.

Words to learn

anther	petal
carpel	pollen
disperse	pollinate
fertilization	reproduction
germinate	sepal
gestation	stamen
life cycle	stigma
ovary	style
ovum	

Skills check

Can you...

- measure length and volume?
- make observations and comparisons?
- explain what you find out?

These salmon are trying to get back to their birthplace

Let's find out...

Salmon live in rivers and the sea. After years at sea they swim back to the river where they were born. After thousands of miles in the sea, then upstream against the river, many become exhausted. They struggle on until they succeed or die. Why do salmon return to their birthplace, even if some die?

Things to learn

- Why we need the Sun.
- What plants need light for.
- How much light a plant needs.

Light and energy

Without the Sun's light it would be very dark and cold. There wouldn't be any plants or animals. Without the energy from the Sun, there wouldn't be life on Earth at all! The Sun provides heat energy, so that the Earth is warm. Even at the North and South Poles the heat from the Sun can **melt** the ice.

Without the Sun there would be no plants. Without plants, there would be no food. The Sun is the start of almost every food chain.

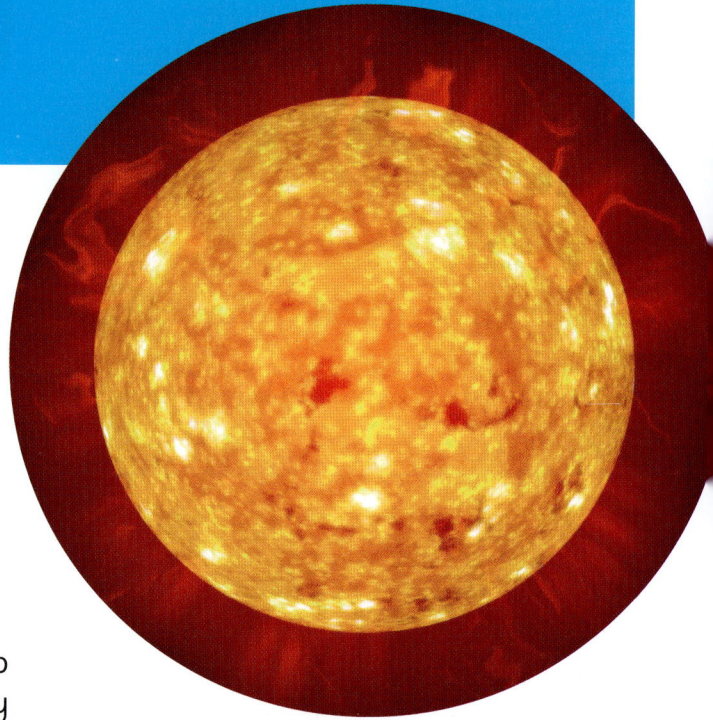

The Sun is the source of the energy for life on Earth

Without the Sun we wouldn't have any of these foods

Plants and light

Plants need energy from the Sun to make food. Plants make sugars which they store as starch. The starch food is stored in their leaves and roots. We eat plants for the starch they have stored. There is starch in all cereals and vegetables we eat. Plants also provide vitamins and minerals.

Things to do

Growing upwards

Plants need light energy from the Sun to make food. How can we prove this?

You need two healthy plants to measure how much they grow.

You need a table to keep your data in. How many columns and rows will you need? You are going to measure the height of two plants every day for two weeks.

- Measure the start height of both plants. Record it in the table.
- Place one plant on the windowsill in full light. It doesn't have to be in direct sunlight.
- Place the other plant on the same windowsill. Make a cylinder of paper or card to go around the pot and the plant. Cover the plant.
- What do you notice after two weeks? Why do you think this is?
- Share your data. Prove your theory to the rest of the class. What other ways could you present the data?

This is one way of finding out if plants need light to grow. Can you think of any others? Why not try them?

I wonder...

Do plants grow in different coloured light? If so, which colour light will plants grow best in?

Dig deeper

Find out:
- if plants can grow in just artificial light (without sunlight)
- what makes a plant's leaves green.

Did you know?

- Over three-quarters of all plant life is in the oceans.

Kelp growing in the sea

New life

Things to learn

- How new plants are made.
- The purpose of a flower and its parts.
- Why insects are important to plants.

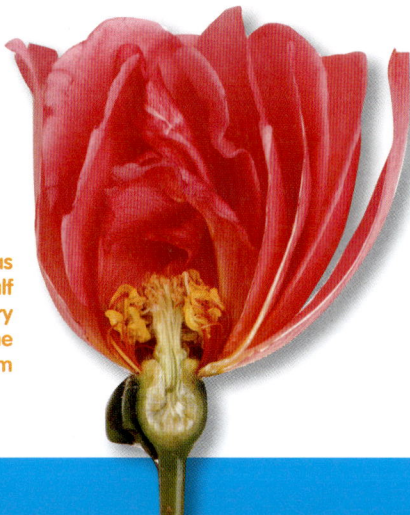
Some flowers attract insects by being brightly coloured

Flowers are useful

A flower isn't there just to look and smell pretty. The plant has a real use for a flower! It is the reproductive part of the plant. It contains both the male and female parts.

Pollination

For a flowering plant to **reproduce**, it has to be **pollinated**. **Pollen** from the male part of the flower must reach the female part of another flower. Very light pollen can be carried on the wind. Insects and some other animals carry pollen from flower to flower. The plants cannot reproduce without them.

Attractive to insects

Some flowers attract insects with their large, colourful **petals**. Some flowers attract with their scent. Insects drink their sweet nectar. Sticky pollen clings to the insect. When the insect moves to another flower, some of the pollen rubs off. It reaches the female parts of the new flower. This is called pollination.

Fertilization

The pollen lands on the female part, the **stigma**, and starts to grow a pollen tube. The male part of the pollen moves down this to the **ovum**, or the egg, in the ovary. Once the male part reaches the ovum, the two join together. This is called **fertilization**. Once the egg has been fertilized it starts to produce a seed.

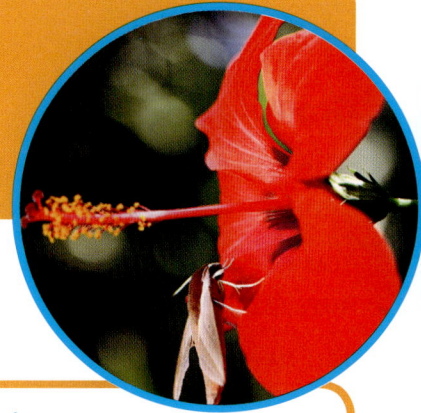
This flower has been cut in half to show the ovary which contains the ovum

What is in a flower?

A flower has a **stamen** and a **carpel**. These are the male and female parts of a flower.

● Look carefully at a large flower. Draw what you see from the outside. Draw from the top looking in. Carefully pull the petals off the flower. Look at the parts inside.

One part stands up slightly higher than the others. This is the female **carpel**. It is made up of a stigma and a **style**. Around the carpel are the male stamens. The long **filament** supports an **anther**. The anther produces pollen.

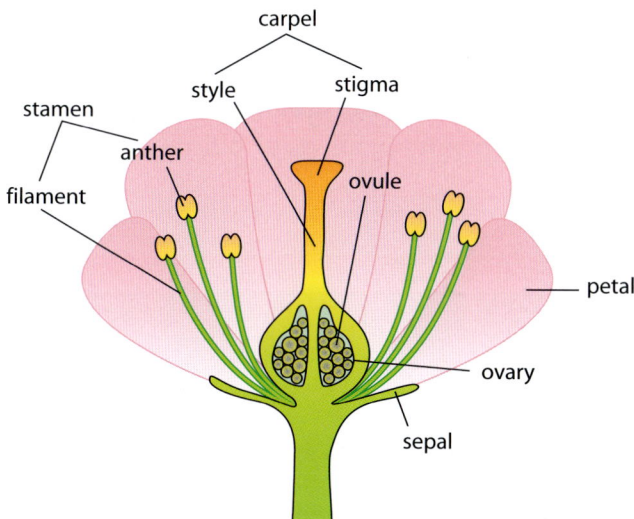

Parts of a flower

I wonder...

The Rafflesia flower smells of rotting meat. It looks like bad meat too! What animals does it attract?

Dig deeper

Find out:
● other methods of pollination
● about the different shapes and types of flowers
● what happens to the fertilized egg.

Did you know?

● Most plant pollen is **flammable**. It ignites and explodes on a hot surface!
● The average pollen grain is smaller than the width of a human hair!
● One ragwort plant can release a billion grains of pollen.

Fruits and seeds

Things to learn
- What the seed of a flowering plant is for.
- How plants scatter their seeds and why they need to do this.

Seed dispersal

Once a plant has developed its seeds in the ovary, it spreads them around or **disperses** them. If they all landed and tried to grow next to the parent plant, they would compete for light, water and space. If you observe plants you will see the ones closest to the parent are smaller. Can you explain why?

How seeds travel

Plants disperse their seeds in different ways. Some have tiny hooks that catch on animal fur. Some are eaten by animals and pass out in their waste. This may be miles away from the parent plant.

Some seeds are carried by the wind or float on water. Others are fired into the air, like an explosion! Each method carries the seed far from the parent plant. The seed can **germinate** and grow into a healthy, new plant.

How can you tell these seeds are being dispersed by the wind?

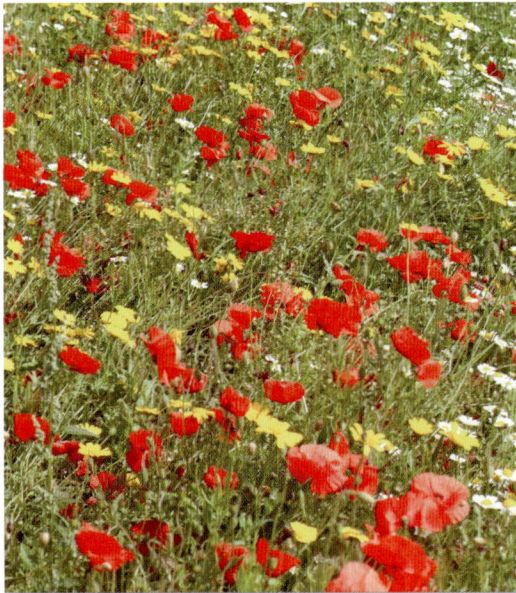

If seeds all land next to the parent plant, there isn't enough room to grow

Animals eat the fruit in one place, and the seeds are passed out in their waste in another place

Things to do

What's inside?

A seed has its own food store. It uses this to send out the first root and then a shoot that grows into a new plant. The plant doesn't need light or to make food to begin its life. It only needs light later on, when it has leaves. This is why seeds can germinate underground.

- Look carefully at a large bean seed. Draw it. Peel the skin off with your fingernail. Inside are two seed leaves. Split them with your fingernail. What can you see? Are other seeds the same?

Know your seeds

Collect many different fruits and seeds. Look closely. Use a hand lens or magnifier. What clues can you find to tell you how the seed is dispersed? Is the seed something you could eat? Is it very light? Does it float? Use your results to create a key. Identify more unusual seeds and the way the parent plant disperses them.

I wonder...

If you drop a satsuma in deep water, what happens? How does this help with its dispersal?

Dig deeper

Find out:
- more about fruits and seeds.

Did you know?

- A million seeds from the orchid flower weigh less than one gram.
- Sesame seeds burst open when they ripen.
- Scientists once grew a plant from a lotus seed that was 10 000 years old!
- George De Mestral, the inventor of Velcro®, got his idea from the hooks on a seed.

Different types of seeds

Investigating seed shapes

Your challenge

- Discover what shape carries a seed furthest in the air.
- Decide how to measure how good the design is.
- Explain which design would be best and why.

It's not fair! My seed only has one small wing.

Why isn't that fair?

It won't go as far as a seed with a bigger one.

Perhaps we should test that idea with paper seeds.

What to do

Some plants produce seeds known as 'helicopters' or flying seeds. These seeds need to travel a long way from the parent plant. Class 5 decided to make some different-shaped and different-sized paper spinners to see which will travel furthest in the air. They need to keep the investigation fair and measure to see which design is best. Here are some of their ideas.

We will change the length of the wings. We think longer wings will turn more slowly.

We want to change the shape of the wing. The longer it takes to fall, the further it can travel.

We will change the length and shape of the wing. We think bigger spinners will take longer to fall.

What you need

- paper
- scissors
- sticky tape
- a stopwatch
- ideally, a video camera

What to check

Now try it yourselves.

- Class 5 have agreed to drop all the spinners from 2 m high. Why?
- Will you use one of their ideas or your own?
- Do you agree with their predictions?

What did you find?

Class 5 kept the shape of the spinner the same and changed the length of the wings. They drew a table of their results.

Length of wing (cm)	Time to fall 2 m (seconds)
10	4.8
5	8.0
8	6.1
12	3.2
16	2.5

- Put your results in a table. Make a graph from it or use Class 5's results. You could use a computer to make your graph. What type of graph could you make? Can you explain why?
- What pattern is there in your results? Which type of spinner took the longest time to fall? Which type of spinner could travel the furthest? Why is this?

Can you do better?

If you dropped each spinner three times from 2 m, what difference would this make to your results? How would you record the results? How would dropping each one five times give you better evidence? Why might it be better to drop the same spinner lots of times?

Now predict

- Class 5J collected a variety of seeds with wings that can be dispersed by the wind. Which ones will fly furthest? How can you tell? Share your ideas.
- Some of the seeds that Class 5J collected have very small wings, but still travel a long way. Devise a test to find out why.
- Use it to explain your ideas to the rest of the class. How will you present your results to prove your test is right?

Germinating seeds

Your challenge

- Identify all the conditions a seed needs to germinate.
- Carry out a fair test.
- Draw a conclusion from your evidence.

What to do

Class 5A want to grow some seeds into plants. This is called germination. They need to know what conditions seeds need to germinate fast. They know the best growing conditions for plants. But do seeds need the same conditions? Which of their suggestions would you choose? Would you do something different?

Do you think anyone has noticed we're here?

They can't have. We haven't any water!

We all have, silly!

Well, I've got my own food supply. I'll be OK.

Yes, but that's not all we need!

What you need

- seeds
- trays
- cotton wool
- measuring cylinders
- a digital camera or a video camera

We want to grow some seeds in the dark and some in the light, with water and warmth.

We will grow some seeds in the dark and some in the light with water but no warmth.

What to check

Now try it yourselves.

- Each group in Class 5A did their own investigation. They counted the number of seeds that had germinated after five days. Why?
- Did they get good-quality results?
- Will you give the seeds any water?

What did you find?

After five days, Class 5A counted the number of seeds that had produced a shoot with leaves. This is called a seedling. They drew a table of the results.

Conditions	Number of seeds germinated
wet, dark and warm	9
wet, dark and cold	6
wet, light and warm	8
wet, light and cold	3
dry, dark, warm	0

- Is 5A's data continuous? This means data with no breaks. Do seeds grow continuously – without a break? If the evidence is continuous, you can draw a line graph. What graph or chart could you draw of Class 5A's results? What kind of chart could you draw of your results? Try using a computer program to draw one, too.
- How does your graph show what conditions seeds need to germinate quickly?
- Make a list of those conditions that are important for germination and those that are not. What do you notice?

Can you do better?

How could you test to see if seeds really don't need light to germinate? Would you get better results if you used 30 seeds instead of 15? Why?

Now predict

- Some Class 5 students are trying to grow some plants from seed. They found that plants like water and warmth, but not how to germinate the seeds. Put together a presentation with images and graphs. Prove what conditions seeds need to germinate.
- Class 5K want to grow some tomato plants for the summer fair, which is only three weeks away! What advice would you give them so the plants will germinate quickly? Produce an instruction leaflet for them.

Life cycles

How species survive

Every plant and animal needs to reproduce. If they don't, that species will die out completely. It will become **extinct**. Adult animals ensure that their offspring have the best chance of survival. They follow a **life cycle**.

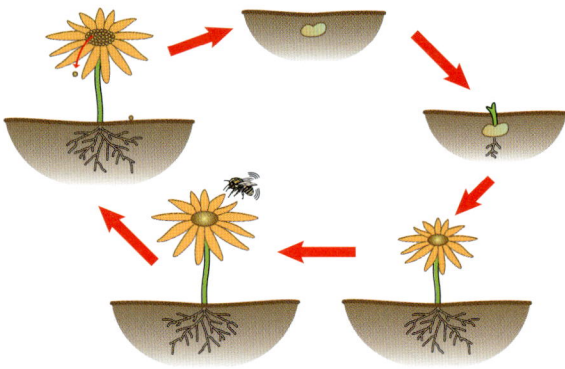

On and on and on…

A seed sends out a root, then a shoot and germinates into a seedling. The seedling grows into a plant, which produces flowers. The flower is pollinated and the ovum fertilized. It produces fruit and seeds. The seeds germinate into seedlings and the cycle begins again. Without the seeds there wouldn't be any new plants. But without flowers there wouldn't be any fruits or seeds!

This is called a life cycle.

Life cycle stages

All animals go through a life cycle, including humans. Some of the stages have different names. An insect will have a stage where they are a larva. The larva **pupates** and becomes an adult. Mammals give birth to live young. Other animals, such as birds and fish, lay eggs. Birth, growth, reproduction and death are part of our life cycle.

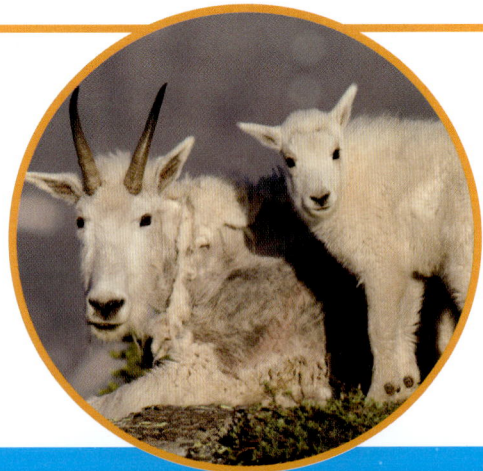

Baby mammals need their parents to look after them

Things to do

The wheel of life

How long do the life cycles of plants and animals take? Life cycles take different lengths of time.

The **gestation** period of an animal is the time from fertilization of the egg to the birth of the **offspring**.

- Find out how long the gestation of various mammals takes. How could you present your data? Think of two ways.
- Which animal has the longest gestation period of all? Why do you think that is?

Human life cycle

As we grow older we learn to do more things. Our parents do less for us.

- Use pictures of your family to build up a life cycle. Where should you start? Place all your pictures in a circle.
- Next to each one write all the new things you can do at that age. Below, in a different colour, write the things your parents do for you. What do you notice about what your parents do for you as you get older?

I wonder...

How good are you at guessing people's ages? What clues are you looking for? How would you trick someone into thinking you were younger than you are?

Dig deeper

Find out:
- more about animal life cycles, including humans
- what happens to a tadpole as it grows older
- what a hen's egg contains.

Did you know?

- The male Darwin frog keeps his tadpoles in his mouth until they are froglets!
- The male seahorse carries his babies round with him in a pouch!
- Human babies naturally grip things put in their hands.

What have you learned?

- Animals and plants reproduce so that their kind can survive.
- Plants need energy from sunlight to grow well.
- Pollination is the transfer of pollen from one flower to another.
- Insects are important in pollination.
- Plant fertilization is the combining of the pollen and egg.
- Seeds and pollen can be dispersed in a variety of ways.
- Seeds don't require the same conditions as plants for growth.
- Animals and plants have life cycles.
- Human children depend on their parents for a long time.

Find out more about...

- other animals' life cycles
- how different plants reproduce.

A female mouse with her brood of baby mice

Check-up

Class 5H have decided to keep some mice. Mice live for about three years. They have a gestation period of about three weeks. Baby mice are blind and helpless. The class want to have two mice.

- Explain what will happen if the mice have a baby of each sex.
- How many generations of mice might the class have after one year?

The answer!

Remember the very first question? Salmon are born in a river and go back there to reproduce. Salmon lay large numbers of unprotected eggs. They rely on numbers, not care, for survival. These eggs need to be in the best place to develop into new fish. The adult salmon survived in its birth river, so will take great risks to lay its eggs there. This will give the new baby salmon the best chance of surviving and growing into adults.

Unit 4: Light

We can see the world around us in the daytime. When it is dark, there is less **light**. Can we see in the dark? How can we see things that don't give out light? Where does most of the light around us come from?

What do you know?

- We need light to see.
- Light comes from a **source**.
- There are many sources of light.
- When there is no light there is darkness.
- It is dangerous to look directly at the Sun.

Skills check

Can you...

- make careful observations and measurements?
- plan a fair test?
- collect evidence and decide how good it is?
- make and repeat careful measurements?
- notice patterns in your results?
- use evidence to try to explain what you've discovered?

Words to learn

beam
block
light
opaque
reflection
shadow
silhouette
source
translucent
transparent
travels

Let's find out...

The Radiation Rangers have their base in the shed at the bottom of Adbul's garden. Their rivals, the Laser Lads, have their base in the garden next door. How can the Rangers see the Lads approaching before their garden is invaded?

Light sources

Things to learn
- Some of the sources of light.
- How light travels from a source.
- If light can be measured.

Brightness of light is measured in lux with a light sensor

Where does light come from?

People used to believe that light came out of our eyes. It lit up things so we could see them. Now we know that our eyes take in light. We have to be careful how bright the light is that we look at. We shouldn't look directly at the Sun because it is too bright. Even looking directly at a torch can hurt your eyes. Scientists can measure how bright a light is and if it is safe to use. They measure this in 'lux' using a light sensor.

The biggest and most important source of light is the Sun. What would our lives be like without the Sun? Light comes from other sources too. Name three more.

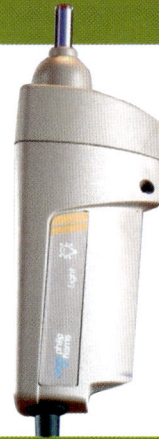

The speed of light

Light takes time to travel. We can measure this. From the Sun, light takes about eight minutes to reach us. That's very fast! It has to travel 148 million kilometres to get here. Light travels 300 000 km in just one second. Nothing travels faster! It is the speed limit for everything in the universe.

How light travels

Light radiates or travels in straight lines from its source. It cannot bend. You can sometimes see straight rays or **beams** of light. They may shine through the leaves in a forest.

Things to do

Go direct

- Look at a torch beam through a long cardboard tube.
- Now bend the tube. Point one end at the light source. Look through the other. What do you see? Use this to demonstrate to another class how light travels. What will you say?

Shadow pictures

Long ago, a Frenchman called Etienne de Silhouette made portraits. He cut out the shape of profiles in black paper. We call these **silhouettes**.

- Make a silhouette. Chalk round your friend's **shadow** on black paper.
- Would this work if light went round corners?
- Can you make a shape look like something else in its silhouette?

I wonder...

Do bulls really see red?

Dig deeper

Find out:
- more about the colour of light
- about the brightness of different places: the stars, your room at home, the school office, etc.

Did you know?

- Deep-sea angler fish make their own light from chemicals in their bodies.
- Insects can see colours that we can't. 'Bee purple' is ultraviolet light. We cannot see ultraviolet light. But bees can!

Blackout blinds

Your challenge

- Find out which material makes the best blackout blind.
- Explore how some materials let lots of light through them and others don't.
- Decide how to measure the amount of light.

What to do

Raj is a baker. He gets up early to bake bread. He goes to bed when it is still light. The Sun shines through his bedroom curtains. His children are testing materials to find the best curtain to **block** out the light.

The fabric with the darkest shadow blocks the most light.

The children sorted the materials into two piles. One pile they thought would block light well and one pile they thought would not block light well.

They held each material between a bright torch and a large piece of white card. They decided which made the darkest shadow.

Every time, they put the material the same distance from the light source. They even tested the materials they thought wouldn't work. Why do you think they did this?

What you need

- a bright torch or other light source
- white card
- a selection of materials to test
- ideally, a light sensor

What to check

Now try the experiment yourselves.

- How are you going to keep the experiment fair?
- How will you decide the darkest shadow?
- Will you need to record anything else about the shadow?
- Which materials do you think will block the most light?

What did you find?

Raj's children put their materials in order. Here are their results, but not in order.

Material	Shade of shadow
thick cardboard	dark
cork tile	dark
fur fabric	dark
foil	dark
writing paper	light
tissue paper	light
plastic sheet	no shadow
cling film	no shadow
greaseproof paper	light

● We call materials that are good at blocking light **opaque**. **Translucent** materials let some light through. **Transparent** materials let almost all of the light through. Add a column to the table. Say what kind of material each is. Use these scientific words.

● Which materials could they use for the curtains? Why?

● What did you notice about the types of material that let light through and those that didn't?

● What can you say about their results? How might they get more accurate results?

● Why is an opaque material the best for making the curtains?

Can you do better?

● How might the results be different if you used a brighter light?

● How do we use opaque, translucent and transparent materials?

Now predict

● The children want to show their friend what they have been doing. Their friend wants to test some materials too. She doesn't have a torch.

● Devise an easy test to show whether something is opaque, translucent or transparent.

● Write a set of instructions.

Changing shadows

Your challenge

- Observe in detail how a shadow is made.
- Find out how you can change the size of shadows.

We'll make six different-sized rockets and change them over really quickly. It will look as if it's the same one getting smaller.

But everyone will see and it won't look real.

What to do

The children are preparing a shadow puppet show. The play is about launching a space rocket to Mars. They want the rocket to look smaller as it moves away from the Earth. Help them make that happen.

Make a cut-out rocket. Measure the distance between it and the light source. How big is its shadow? How can you record its size?

Draw around the outline of the rocket on a card screen each time.

One student wanted to colour in the rockets so the shadow would be coloured. Why won't this work?

What you need

- a bright torch or other light source
- a white card screen
- a cut-out rocket
- metre rulers

What to check

Now you try it.

- Which distance are you going to measure? Is that fair?
- Predict before you start. What do you think the children found?
- Instead of drawing round the rocket shadow, what else could you measure? What happens when you change the distances?

Why don't we try moving the rocket or the light source?

What difference will that make?

What did you find?

The children drew around each shadow and measured its height. Here are their results.

Distance from light (cm)	Height of shadow (cm)
6	53
8	46
10	39
20	33
30	31
40	30
50	29
60	28
70	27
80	27
90	27
100	26

- Draw a table of your evidence or use the children's results. Use a computer program to help you.
- Write the story of your graph. When was the shadow smallest? How far away from the light was the rocket to make the biggest shadow?

- Draw a picture to show why you think the shadows changed like this.
- Can you see a pattern between the distance of the rocket and the light source against the size of the shadow?

Can you do better?

- How good is your evidence? If you did this again, would you do anything differently?
- The children noticed other changes to the shadows they made. They didn't just change size. What else do you think they noticed?

Now predict

- Class 3 enjoyed the puppet show very much. They want to put on their own show. What advice would you give them? Write a helpful set of instructions. Use pictures to help.
- Mansoor's little sister wants to make shadows, but she doesn't like the dark. Can she make shadows with the light on? How could you explain and demonstrate this?

Sunlight and shadows

Your challenge

- Observe how shadows are made by the Sun.
- Find out how shadows change throughout the day.
- Measure and record the length of a shadow.
- Measure and record the direction of a shadow.

Never take a photograph of the Sun directly! It could seriously damage your eyesight.

I know that shadows are made when light from the Sun is blocked.

If I stand in the Sun a shadow will form.

The shadow is always on the side facing away from the Sun.

The position of the shadow should change with the position of the Sun.

What to do

Plan an investigation to show how the shadow of an object changes during the day.

What you need

- a sunny day
- an opaque object – a stick or pole, or a pop bottle full of sand
- a measuring stick
- chalk
- a digital camera

What to check

- Which distance will you measure?
- Is it fair?
- When are you going to make your measurements?
- How are you going to record your measurements?

Let's record some shadow postitions each hour.

We can draw the shadow we make and measure how it changes.

What did you find?

The students in Class 5 stood a stick in the school yard. Why do you think they did that? They drew around its shadow every hour and measured its length. This is what they found.

As the children recorded the shadow during the day, a pattern appeared on the ground

Time of day	Length of shadow (cm)
9.00	19
10.00	9
11.00	1
12.00	9
1.00	18
2.00	33
3.00	55

- Use a computer program to draw a chart of your results or use Class 5's results.
- Write the story of your graph. When did the longest shadows appear? When did you find the shortest shadows? Where was the Sun at these times? Describe what happens to the shadows during the day.
- Model this in the classroom with a torch and stick.

Can you do better?

- How good is your evidence? If you did this again what would you do differently?

Now predict

- Use your evidence. Predict where the shadows of the stick would be every half hour and what they would look like. Draw this as a picture.
- If you had a drawing of a shadow, how could you point to the position of the Sun? Set a challenge for your friends. Ask them to work out the Sun's position from your shadow and stick drawings. Can you think of a rule for this?

How we see things

Things to learn

- How our eyes see things.
- How scientists show how we see.
- How light is important to help us see.

Scattered sunlight

Not everything we see is a light source. When light hits an object, the object absorbs some of the light energy. The rest either passes straight through the object (if it is transparent) or bounces back. Light that bounces back is reflected. Light hitting rough surfaces such as wood, stone, paper or wool will bounce off in all directions. The light has been **scattered**. They will appear dull. Smooth objects look shiny.

The Moon is not a light source. It reflects and scatters the light from the Sun.

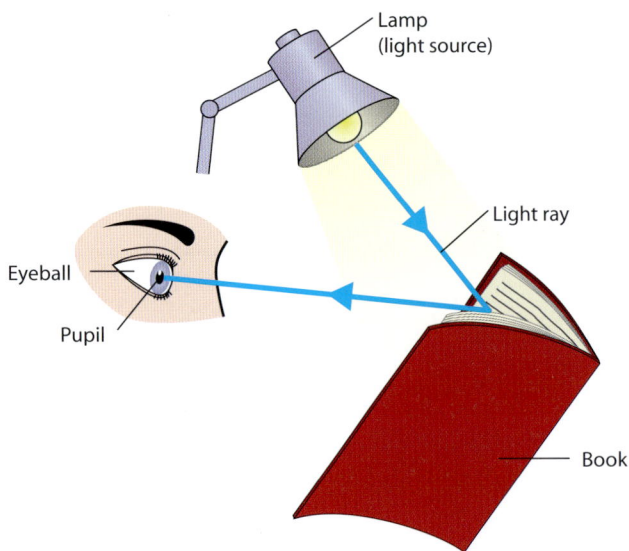

We see when light is reflected from the book

Windows to the world

Our eyes are our windows to the world. Light enters our eyes from outside so that we can see. How?

We see the Sun, the stars, fireworks and car headlights because they are all light sources. Light travels in straight lines at very high speed from the source. It bounces or reflects from objects and enters our eyes.

To be able to see, the light enters our eyes through the pupil (the black hole in the centre of your eye).

Light-sensitive cells at the back of your eyes receive the light and send messages to your brain. It **interprets** them so that you 'see' and recognize the object.

Things to do

Shiny or dull?

When light hits an object it bounces off and changes direction. Shiny objects reflect light well. Most of the light bounces or reflects in a single direction. Do you think there are more shiny or dull objects in your classroom?

- Shine a beam of light from a torch on different objects in a darkened room. What do you notice about how the light is reflected?
- Draw a table to record whether the object is shiny or dull. It may reflect light well or scatter it.

Light rays

We can represent rays of light as straight lines with arrows on them. The arrow shows the direction of the light ray.

- Draw diagrams of your objects to show how the light behaves, using lines and arrows.
- Which way should the arrows be pointing? Why?
- Now draw a diagram showing how you 'see' the object.

I wonder...
Can you see in the dark? How can you find out?

Bright or dark

Cover your eyes with your hands and get your partner to watch you. Quickly remove your hands and ask them to look at your pupils.

- What do they notice? Now look at their eyes.
- Why do you think this happens?

Dig deeper
Find out:
- more about the human eye and how we see
- about **binocular vision**.

Did you know?

- The muscles in your eyes adjust around 100 000 times every day.
- The object you see is upside down in your eye. Your brain turns it the right way.
- If you are out in very dim light, then it is very hard to see in colour.

Reflection

Things to learn

- How we see things.
- How to change the direction of light.
- What happens when a ray of light hits a mirror or other reflective surface.

How mirrors work

Polished, smooth or shiny surfaces bounce light rays back all in the same direction. Rough surfaces scatter them. That's why we see an image in a mirror.

How many things can you think of that reflect light?

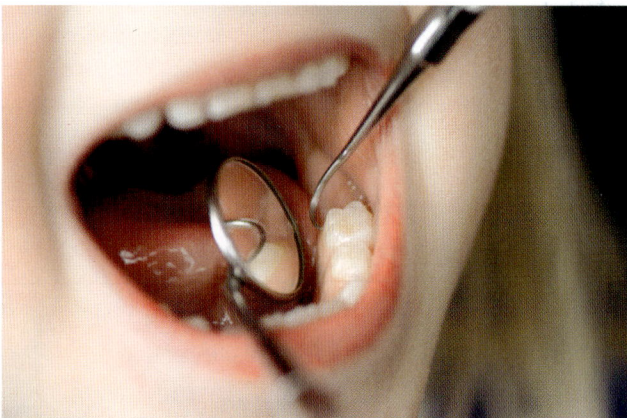

Mirrors can help us see things in awkward places. Who else might use a mirror to help them?

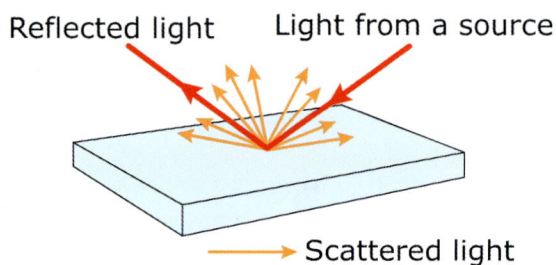

Reflected light   Light from a source

Scattered light

Bending light

Light travels very fast in straight lines. We can make it 'bend' though! A 'bend' is a change of direction. We make light change direction when it is reflected. A mirror is a very reflective surface that is good at this.

Dentists use tiny mirrors in our mouths to see our back teeth. The light enters our mouth, hits the tooth and is bounced off. It travels to the mirror where it is reflected and then travels to the dentist's eye. The light has changed direction from entering our mouth to leaving it! This is another **reflection**.

Things to do

Make a mirror

- A smooth sheet of aluminium foil acts like a mirror. Crease it, and it still reflects light. Why can't you see your face in it now?

What can you see?

Where is the best place to stand if you want to see your reflection? Most people will stand facing the mirror. What happens if you stand to one side? Try it.

- Draw a diagram showing how the light travels from the source to the mirror then to your eyes. Use arrows for the light rays.

I wonder...

Why are the words 'Police' and 'Ambulance' painted back-to-front on some police cars and ambulances?

Target practice

- Place a 'target' on the wall or floor. Face away from it. Hold a mirror in your hand. Reflect the light with the mirror. Hit the target using the reflection to guide you.

Did you know?

- The Keck telescope in Hawaii has a curved mirror 10 m across. It gathers the faint light from distant stars.
- American astronauts left a mirror on the Moon to reflect a laser beam sent from Earth 400 000 km away!

What have you learned?

- The Sun is our most important source of light.
- Light travels in straight lines.
- How shadows are made and what they look like.
- How shadows can be changed.
- What transparent, translucent and opaque objects can do to light.
- You can measure the amount of light.
- How to measure and record shadows.
- How we see when light enters our eyes.
- How you can change the direction of light with a mirror.
- Shiny surfaces reflect light better than dull surfaces.
- How shadows change during the day.

Find out more about…

- how other animals see
- how to use a mirror to signal someone a long way off
- safety and the Sun. How can the Sun be dangerous for us?

Check-up

Nishi is relaxing on the beach.

- What would be the best material for a parasol? Why?
- Why is Nishi wearing sunglasses?
- How can Nishi see her sister when she is lying on her lounger?

Why can you see your reflection in a still pool of water but not on the rough sea?

The answer!

Do you remember the question about how the Radiation Rangers could see the Laser Lads coming? One early warning system would be to mount mirrors on trees so the Rangers could 'see round corners'. The images of the Lads would be reflected in the mirrors. The images would bounce at an angle so that the Rangers could see them. They might use mirrors to make a periscope and see over the garden hedge without being seen.

Unit 5: Changing state

Have you had a drink of tap water recently? That water has been used many times before it reached you. Water can be cleaned and reused. Water **evaporates** and **condenses**.

What do you know?

- Materials can be grouped as solids, liquids or gases.
- Solids have a fixed shape.
- Liquids take the shape of their container. They can be poured. They have a flat top.
- Gases have no shape. They fill the space available.
- Solids **melt** to become liquids.
- Liquids **freeze** at low temperatures to become solids.

Words to learn

boiling point	melt
condense	solidify
change of state	spin
evaporate	vapour
freeze	water cycle

Skills check

Can you…

- make careful observations and measurements?
- collect evidence and see how good it is?
- explain what you've found out?
- predict something you don't yet know?

Let's find out…

'I think it has stopped raining,' said five-year-old Anya. Her elder brother Devan was looking at a puddle. It was misty just above its surface. 'It's not stopped for long,' he said. 'The next lot of rain is on the way!'

Was Devan right? How did he know? Why might it rain again later?

Evaporation

Things to learn

- What happens when water evaporates.
- Whether liquids other than water evaporate.
- Whether all of a liquid evaporates or if something is left behind.

Solid and liquid

Every winter the Zanskar river in the Himalayas freezes over completely. The ice is so thick that groups of people go trekking along it. The liquid water in the river has turned into a solid. It has **solidified**. When spring arrives, the solid water melts into a liquid again and the river flows.

When you have a bath or shower, the bathroom 'steams up'. The air is filled with tiny droplets of water that we call 'steam'. These droplets come from your bath and from you. The water from your bath has **evaporated** so that the liquid water has turned into water vapour. Water can be solid, liquid or gas, depending on the temperature.

What's in a cloud?

If you have been in an aeroplane, then you probably flew through a cloud. You may have walked through one, as mist or fog. Clouds, fogs and mists are water vapour. Tiny water particles float in the atmosphere or roll across hills.

Evaporation and smells

You can tell when someone is painting their nails. As the varnish is painted on nails, it dries. It leaves colour on the nails and a smell in the air.

Drying is when particles are being lost from the surface of a liquid. This is called evaporation, and we say the liquid is evaporating.

New paint smells, too. It stops smelling when all the liquid has evaporated. Water doesn't smell – if it did, clouds would smell too!

The Zanskar river freezes every winter

Things to do

Puddle puzzle

- Pour water on a hard, waterproof surface outside. Chalk round the puddle it makes. Go back an hour later and chalk round it again. Then again after another hour. What is happening to the puddle? Explain this using the words: evaporation, liquid, gas and vapour.
- Look at your chalk marks. When did the puddle lose most water – early, or later? Why?
- How could you speed up the puddle drying? Look at puddles on hot days, windy days and cooler days without any wind. What do you notice?

Dirty marks

When a liquid evaporates, the liquid particles are escaping. But what happens if the liquid is a solution, such as tea or seawater? Why do we get dirty marks on a teacup if it is not washed up? Why do we get a salty crust if seawater is left to dry in a dish?

- Pour some cold tea into one dish and some salt water solution into another.
- Leave them in a warm place for a week. Then observe the dishes carefully and record what you see.

- What has happened to the solutions? What has evaporated and what is left behind?
- Suggest further tests you could do to support your explanations. What factors would you need to consider?

I wonder...

What are the bubbles in boiling water? Are they water gas? What will happen if we continue to boil the water?

Dig deeper

Find out:
- more about evaporation and how it can be used.

Did you know?

- In some countries, there is always water in the air. It is hard to see on misty mornings. It is hard to see great distances. In hot, dry countries, you can see things far in the distance. Colours are sharper too.

Investigating evaporation

Your challenge

- Explore how differences in containers change the speed of evaporation.
- Make your test fair.
- Explain your results from what you know about evaporation.

I have to water these plants near the window every day. The plant in the hall is never that thirsty!

I don't understand it.

Maybe it's not the plants, Mum. I think it's the plant pot that matters!

What you need

- different water containers
- water
- a measuring cylinder

What to check

Now try it yourselves

- Does it matter how much water you put in each container?
- Where will you put your containers?
- What will you need to keep the same?
- How often will you check the water level?
- How can you measure the evaporation?
- What other factors would you need to consider if you did this investigation at home?

Ajay wanted to discover why the plants in the shallow pot seemed to need a lot more water than the plant in the deep pot.

What to do

Compare the way water evaporates from several different containers. You could use plant pots like Ajay. But it might be quicker if you used something smaller with less water!

I'll put the same amount of water in each container.

What did you find?

Ajay found that the shape of the container made a difference to the speed of evaporation. He decided to measure the diameter of each of his containers.

Much more water had evaporated from the tray than from the thin vase. Ajay looked at the surface of the water. No wonder so little had gone from the vase!

● Why do you think Ajay got these results? Are they like yours?

I think I know what is happening.

Container	Diameter of container (cm)	Volume of water at the beginning (cm³) (a)	Volume of water after one week (cm³) (b)	Volume of water that evaporated (cm³) (a - b)
bowl	20	500	450	50
pot	15	500	400	100
tall jar	10	500	480	20
thin vase	5	500	490	10
tray	30	500	350	150

Can you do better?

How good is your evidence? Can you see a pattern in your results?

How could you work out the surface area of water in each container? Would squared paper help? How could you graph the amount of water lost against the surface area of the containers?

Explain why it would be a good idea to repeat the investigation on a cloudy day, or on a cold day.

Now predict

● Particles of water escape one by one from the surface of a liquid. They are a little like aeroplanes taking off from a busy airport. The bigger the airport, the more planes can take off. Why does the area of the surface matter?
● Make up a short play to explain to your class what happens.

Graphing evaporation

Your challenge

- Investigate the factors that affect the speed of evaporation.
- Control the factors to find out which make a difference.
- Plan a fair test.
- Decide which evidence to collect.

Amani, peg out the washing for me!

But Mum, I'm busy. And it won't dry today, anyway.

Nonsense. It's a perfect day for drying the washing. Warm, with a bit of a breeze. You'll see.

What you need

- several identical pieces of damp fabric
- a washing line
- clothes pegs
- a hand fan; you could use a hairdryer— but DO NOT use it near water!

What to check

Now try it yourselves.

- How will you keep your test fair?
- What will you measure?
- Which factor will you change?
- How will you decide how dry the washing is?
- How will you check and record your results?

I could hang them in different places — warm and cold. I could use a hairdryer on some.

What to do

It is hot and breezy. Amani has hung out her washing. Some days are better than others for drying. Amani wonders why the weather matters. Why is one day better than another? A rainy day is no good, of course. But otherwise, the washing just dries as water evaporates from it. She has learned that at school.

What did you find?

Amani poured one saucer of water over each piece of fabric. She hung her washing in different places around the house. She put it in warm and cold places. She made sure none of the places was in a draught. Then she left it overnight.

● Which was the best place to put the washing? Think of some reasons why.

Where I put the washing	How wet at the start	How wet in the morning	How wet in the afternoon	How wet in the evening
window	soaking	dripping	wet	damp
fridge	soaking	dripping	wet and cold	wet and cold
warm kitchen	soaking	wet	damp	dry
outside	soaking	wet	dry	dry

Where I put the washing	Temperature (°C)
window	16
fridge	4
warm kitchen	20
outside	23

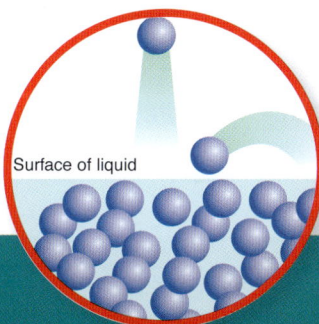

Surface of liquid

Evaporation happens when a particle escapes from the surface of the liquid into the surrounding air

Can you do better?

Amani wondered what the temperature was in her test places. She used a thermometer to find out. Her measurements are in the second table.

Now predict

● Amani tested different places. She did not test the effect of a breeze or moving air. How could she do this? What results would you expect? Why? Add extra rows to Amani's table to predict your results.

Condensation

Things to learn

- The change of state involved in the process of condensation.
- When condensation occurs.
- Some examples of condensation happening around you all the time.

Bath time

Many bathrooms are fitted with extractor fans. These pull the air out of the bathroom. But don't worry! More air takes its place by being pulled under the door! The air that is extracted can be very wet. It is full of water vapour that evaporated as you had your shower and dried yourself. The new air is drier. The extractor fan helps stop the bathroom 'steaming up'.

The water vapour in the air cools on the cold mirror and turns into liquid water

Faces on the mirror

Without an extractor fan, the bathroom can get steamed up. Water in the air **condenses** where it meets a surface that is cold, like the mirror. Condensed water collects and runs down windows and mirrors. It sometimes runs down the walls. You can draw faces in the condensation!

Forwards and backwards

Your bathroom is full of science! The liquid water comes out of the tap. The water is hot and starts to evaporate, turning it into a vapour. The gas then meets a cold surface and condenses. It turns back into a liquid, which we have to wipe up!

Things to do

Where does the water come from?

- Fill a jar with cold water and ice. Screw the lid on. Leave the jar for a while. You will find water on the outside of the jar. Where has it come from? Is the jar leaking?
- Wipe the jar dry. Now breathe on the sides. Where has this new water come from?

In the rainforest the air is full of water vapour. It feels very humid

Water in the desert

- If you guessed that the water on the jar came from the air, you were right. Remember this if you are ever in the desert without water. It turns very cold at night, and water vapour called dew condenses on cold surfaces.
- Try making a desert water collector. Don't drink the water. It may not be clean.

I wonder…

Water condenses. Do other liquids condense, too? Do other liquids and gases freeze like water?

Dig deeper

Find out:
- more about condensing.

Did you know?

- When water evaporates, it leaves behind anything that is dissolved in it. We use evaporation to collect salt from seawater. If the water later condenses again, it will be pure.
- The white smoke that you sometimes see at the theatre is dry ice, or frozen carbon dioxide. At room temperature it melts in a spectacular way.

Solid carbon dioxide is called dry ice

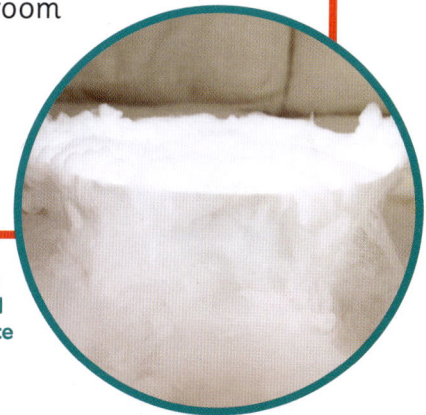

Investigating boiling and freezing

Your challenge

- Investigate the melting of ice and the freezing point of water.
- Accurately measure temperature using a thermometer or a temperature sensor.
- Present your results as a line graph.

The thermometer got stuck, didn't it?

I don't think so. The water was boiling. I think the water reached a sort of stopping point.

*That's right, it reached its **boiling point** – 100°C.*

Mr Haj showed his class an investigation where water was heated with a thermometer in it. Every 60 seconds he called out the temperature: '50°C... 55°C... 60°C...' The students saw the pattern. They guessed the next few readings. But as the water got hotter, they had a surprise. '90°C,' called Mr Faraday. '100°C... 100°C... 100°C...' It got no hotter. The students wondered if the same happened when ice melted to water.

What to do

The students decide to test some ice.

We can record the temperature as the ice melts!

We could test the ice with a thermometer.

A computer sensor would be even better.

What you need

- a container of crushed ice
- a thermometer or temperature sensor connected to a thermometer
- a timer

What to check

Now try it yourselves.

- Take the temperature of the melting ice every minute. Set the computer to do this for you.
- Notice when the ice has become water. What is the temperature?

What did you find?

The students discovered that all the ice became water at close to 0°C. They decided that this was the melting – and freezing – point of water.

Then they got a surprise. The temperature kept on going up, like this:

Time (minutes)	0	1	2	3	4	5	6	7	8	9	10
Temperature (°C)	-2	-2	-1	0	0	2	4	7	10	13	16

What was happening? When would the water stop getting warmer? Would it boil?

'Of course not,' said Mr Haj. 'But I can guess when the temperature will stop rising.' And he looked at the thermometer on the classroom wall.

'At room temperature!' said Harbinder. 'What do you mean – room temperature?' asked Zinah.

🔴 Draw a line graph of your results. Put the minutes on the x-axis and the temperature on the y-axis. What do you notice? When does your graph flatten out? Why?

Can you do better?

How good is your evidence? Would it be better to record freezing rather than melting? Why is that more difficult to do?

Find out about Anders Celsius, the Swedish **astronomer**. Why is he remembered for his temperature scale? What was his original boiling point of water?

Now predict

Keisha left her hot dinner and her ice cream on the table while she answered the telephone. By the time she got back, her dinner had gone cold and her ice cream had melted. What had happened? Can you predict what temperature they were?

The water cycle

Things to learn

- Water is constantly recycled through the water cycle.
- Water evaporates, becomes clouds, condenses and falls as rain.
- The water cycle purifies water for us to use again and again.
- Condensation is the reverse of evaporation.

What a state

We have found out that if you heat ice it melts and forms a liquid called water. If you keep heating the water, it boils and forms a gas. If we cool the gas, it goes back to being a liquid. And if we cool the liquid it goes back to being a solid again. Water isn't the only material to do this, but it is the most important to us.

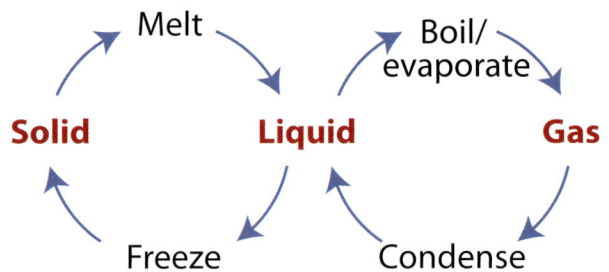

Melt → Boil/evaporate

Solid   **Liquid**   **Gas**

Freeze   Condense

How the states of matter are linked together

Down came the rain

Air contains water vapour. As the air rises and cools water condenses, droplets run together to form bigger and bigger drops. Eventually, these drops become too big to hang in the air. They fall as rain. This usually happens high up. Rain is more likely to fall over mountains or hills, or close to them.

This process is called the **water cycle**.

If the water vapour freezes, it falls as snowflakes. If water droplets are carried higher into colder air, they may freeze. More water gathers round the frozen particles, forming hailstones. They fall to Earth.

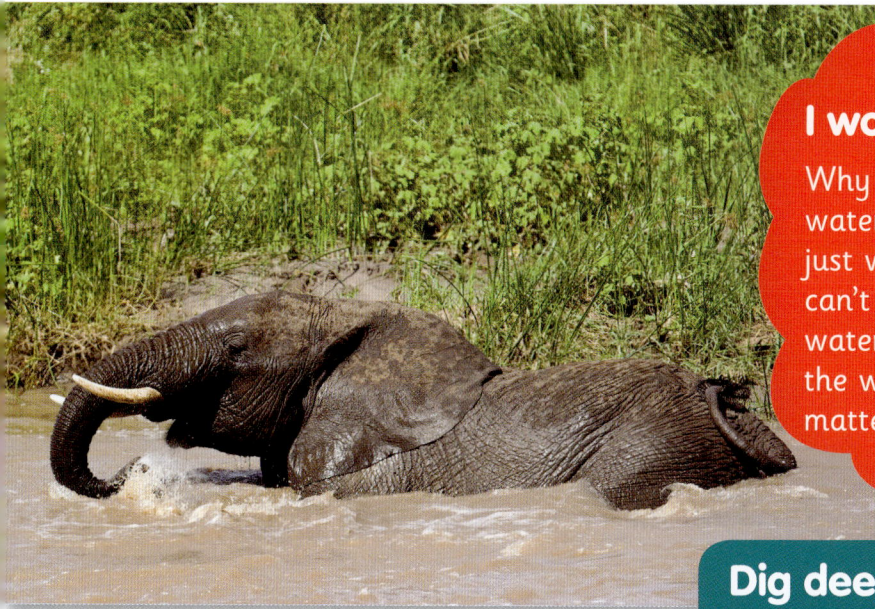

I wonder...

Why do elephants bathe in water on hot days? Do they just want to get clean? They can't get clean in muddy water! Maybe it's the way the water evaporates that matters.

Dig deeper

Find out:
- more about the water cycle
- about the difference between boiling and evaporation.

Things to do

Rain in a bag

Make a cloud in a clear sandwich bag.

- Pour a little water into the bottom of the bag. Fold the top over several times. Seal it and tape the top of the bag to a sunny window. Leave it for a while.
- Some water remains in the bottom. A cloud forms in the bag. Rain collects at the top of the bag. Occasionally, it drips.

Condensing is the reverse of evaporating.

Did you know?

- On average, 10 cm of snow melts to just 1 cm of water.
- In 1939 in Hyderabad, India, hailstones weighing 3.5 kg fell to Earth.
- In 1843, 83 people and 3000 cattle were killed by a hailstorm in the Himalayas.

What have you learned?

- Water can be a solid, a liquid or a gas.
- When liquid water freezes, it becomes ice. When it melts, it becomes water again. The process is reversible.
- When water evaporates, it becomes water vapour. When it condenses, it becomes liquid water again. The process is reversible.
- When water evaporates from a solution, the solid is left behind.
- Liquids evaporate faster when they are warmer and when they have a bigger surface.
- Evaporation cools the surface the liquid evaporates from.
- Water vapour condenses onto cold surfaces to become liquid again.
- The boiling point of water is 100°C (Celsius). The freezing point of water is 0°C (Celsius).
- Water evaporates, forms clouds, condenses and falls as rain in the water cycle.

Find out more about…

- how water can exist as a solid, a liquid and a gas all at once!

Check-up

The survivors in a lifeboat were surrounded by seawater. But they couldn't drink it! They collected the rain that fell in clean containers. Then the Captain stopped them. 'You can't drink that!' he said. 'It won't be clean!' Was he right?

The answer!

Do you remember the first question about whether it might rain again? Devan was right! Water endlessly cycles from the Earth to the sky and back again in the water cycle.

Unit 6: The Earth and beyond

Have you ever looked up at the sky at night and wondered what was up there? **Space** begins where Earth's atmosphere ends, but nobody knows where space ends. Scientists believe that about 15 billion years ago there was a gigantic explosion. The universe was formed.

What do you know?

- We live on a planet called Earth.
- Earth is lit and warmed by the Sun.
- The **Moon** is Earth's natural satellite.

Words to learn

astronomer	satellite
axis	space
constellation	sphere
crescent	sunrise
Moon	sunset
orbit	waning
phase	waxing
planet	

Skills check

Can you...

- make careful observations and measurements?
- collect evidence and see how good it is?
- explain what you've found out?
- predict something you don't yet know?
- recognize that sometimes it is difficult to collect evidence to test scientific ideas?

Let's find out...

Vijay and Mohan were camping in their back garden. They lay on the ground looking up at the stars in the night sky. Vijay noticed that a bright star had disappeared behind the wall of their house. Why had that happened?

Our solar system

Celestial spheres

People in many ancient cultures, including Arabs, Greeks and Mesopotamians once believed that the Earth was flat. If they sailed too far out they might fall off the edge of the world! Now we know that the Earth is a slightly squashed **sphere**. It is a little flatter at the poles than around the middle. The Sun, Moon and **planets** are all spheres too.

Measuring the Earth

About 2500 years ago, Greek **astronomers** calculated the shape and size of the Earth. They couldn't see the whole Earth. They used what they could see to work out that the Earth was round.

When the Earth moves between the Sun and the Moon it casts a circular shadow on the Moon. The only shape that always casts a circular shadow is a sphere.

The Ancient Greeks were great sailors. They noticed that when a ship came over the horizon they didn't see all of it at once. First they saw the top of the mast, and then gradually the rest of the ship. They worked out that the surface of the Earth must be curved. How else could you prove that the Earth is a sphere?

Things to do

How big? How far?

If you were making a model and used a large beach ball to represent the Sun, what would you use for the Earth and the Moon? How far from the Sun would they be?

- Use the space facts in the table to model the solar system.

Name	Diameter (km)	Distance from Sun (millions of km)	Number of known moons
Sun	1 392 000	0	–
Mercury	4820	58	0
Venus	12 103	108	0
Earth	12 756	152	1
Mars	6794	228	2
Jupiter	142 800	778	16
Saturn	120 660	1427	17
Uranus	51 400	2870	15
Neptune	49 400	4497	8

Never look directly at the Sun even when wearing sunglasses; it can damage your eyes.

Dig deeper

Find out:
- about Pluto and the other dwarf planets
- information to build a fact file on your favourite planet.

Did you know?

- If you could fly at the speed of light you could circle the Earth seven times in one second.
- If you filled your classroom with sand, there would be fewer grains of sand than the number of stars in the universe.
- Many of the stars we see have ancient Arabic names.

I wonder...

How long it would take to travel to the Sun?

The Earth, Sun and Moon

Things to learn

- The Sun's place in our solar system.
- How to measure forces.
- How the Moon compares to the Earth.

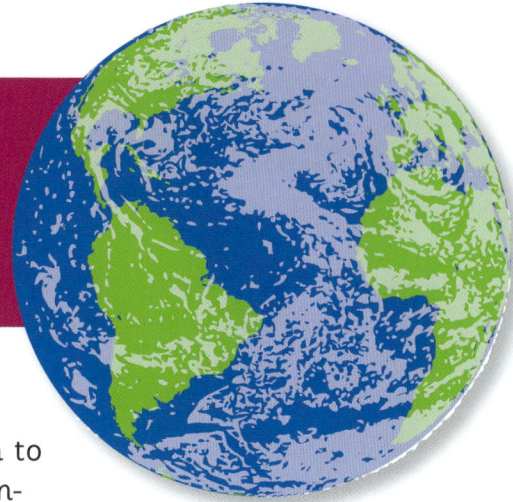

The Earth is over 70 per cent water, and also has an atmosphere containing oxygen for all living things to breathe

The Earth

The Earth is the only planet in our solar system known to have life on it. It has enough gravity to keep an oxygen-rich atmosphere around it. The Earth also has water, essential to all living things.

Our own star

The Sun is the closest star to Earth. It is a ball of gases, mainly hydrogen and helium. They burn to make heat and light. At the Sun's centre the temperature is 15 million°C. Its surface is 6000°C. That's sixty times hotter than boiling water!

In our solar system all the planets **orbit** the Sun. Astronomers use telescopes to study how the planets move around the Sun.

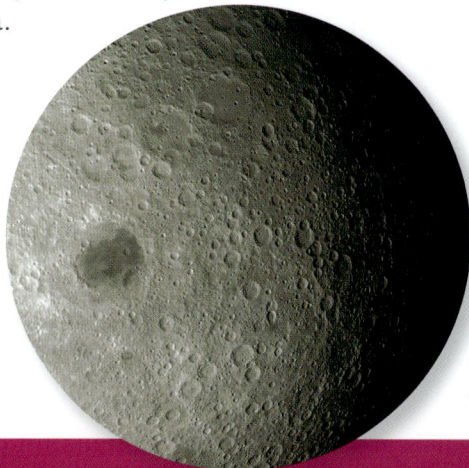

The surface of the Moon is very rocky

What is the Moon?

The Moon is the Earth's natural **satellite** and nearest neighbour. It is a sphere made of a rock, marked with craters. There are no plants or animals on the Moon because there is no air. The Moon is about one-sixth the size of Earth. It looks large in the sky because it is much closer than the stars.

American astronauts in the space rocket Apollo II travelled the 348 000 kilometres to the Moon and landed on it on 20 July 1969. It is the only place in space, other than Earth, that people have visited.

Because the Moon's gravity is so small compared to Earth's, walking becomes jumping!

I wonder...

How much weaker the Moon's gravity is than the Earth's?

Dig deeper

Find out:
- more about what Nicolaus Copernicus discovered
- how often the Earth orbits the Sun.

Things to do

Gravity

The Moon travels in an orbit around the Earth. Earth's gravity pulls the Moon towards us and keeps it at a fixed distance away. The Earth's gravity is six times stronger than the Moon's. But how much do things weigh on the Moon compared to Earth?

Plan a table to record your information. Choose a measuring device to help you. How can you work out how much something weighs on the Moon? What information helps you?

Did you know?

- The Japanese call their country 'Nippon' which means 'origin of the Sun'.
- The ancient Mayan people made a calendar to predict the postion of the Sun through the year.
- The ancient Egyptians used a 365¼ day calendar like we do today, only their calendar existed 1600 years ago!

Our turning Earth

Your challenge

- Model how the Earth spins on its axis.
- Explore whether it is the Sun or the Earth that moves.
- Demonstrate night and day in different parts of the world.

What to do

Minah and Sahem's father had gone on a business trip on the other side of the world. How could Minah explain to Sahem why it was night-time where their father was?

Why can't I phone Dad now?

Because he's on the other side of the world. He'll be asleep.

He can't be sleeping. It's the middle of the day!

Not where he is. It's night-time there!

The Earth **spins** anticlockwise round its **axis**. It spins round once every 24 hours.

So as the Earth spins, sometimes Dad is in the light and sometimes we are.

Yes, so when it's day on one side of the world it's night on the other.

What you need

- a spinning globe
- a torch or strong light source
- card
- sticky tape

What to check

The torch is the Sun. Shine it at the Earth.

- Make sure that your Sun doesn't move when the Earth spins.
- Which direction does our Earth actually spin?
- How else could you show how we get night and day?

What did you find?

Sahem was interested in the way the Earth moved in space. He marked the position of the Sun on his bedroom window at different times of the day. Every day it rose in the east and set in the west. It looked as if the Sun was moving. Sahem knew that it was really the Earth spinning that made it seem that way.

Sahem noticed that as the Sun's position changed, the length and direction of shadows seemed to change. He put a stick in the ground outside and made these drawings of the shadow every two hours.

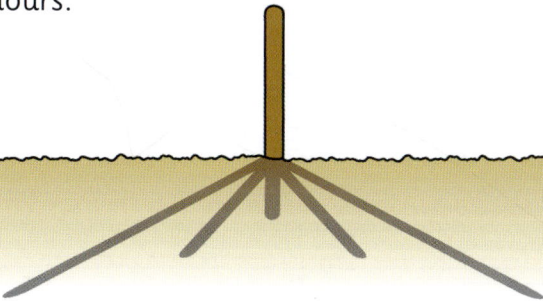

- Carry out this investigation and draw a chart of your results.
- Write the story of your chart. When did the longest shadows appear? When did you find the shortest shadows? Where was the Sun at these times?
- Think back to your topic on light. Can you explain what is happening?

Can you do better?

How good is your evidence? Could your evidence mean something else? How well do your models explain how the Earth moves?

What factors have to be taken into account by someone doing this investigation in Russia, compared with someone doing it in India?

Now predict

Sahem noticed that although the Sun rose and set in the same direction every day, the time it rose and set was slightly different each day. Why was that? Draw a sketch. Show how the position of the Sun changes. Write a caption underneath to explain it.

Things to learn

- Science has a long history. Many people from different cultures have contributed.
- How scientists use their careful observations and measurements.
- How scientists use their imagination to question and explain the evidence they collect.

Ancient Egyptians

The ancient Egyptians believed that the Sun was a god named Ra-Atum-Khepri. The three names stood for the three stages of the day: Khepri means 'rising Sun', Ra means 'Sun at noon' and Atum means 'setting Sun'. They thought the god was rowing a boat across the sky.

These ideas came from their observations of the Sun. It appeared to move across the sky during the day.

Then came the Greeks

Over 2400 years ago, the Greek philosopher Aristotle considered how the Earth and the Sun moved together. He suggested that the Sun and other planets orbited around the Earth.

His evidence was that the Sun, Moon and stars all appeared to circle the Earth in the sky. The Earth didn't appear to move. It felt solid to everyone on it.

But he didn't explain why some planets appear to go backwards when you watch them in the sky!

Further developments

Around 1500 years ago the famous Indian astronomer Aryabhata suggested that the Earth was moving. He said it was spinning on its axis. That was how we had day and night.

Many Muslim astronomers also tried to prove this. They observed the planets at the Maragheh observatory over 800 years ago. The work of astronomer Nasir al-Din al-Tusi was used by Nicolaus Copernicus 300 years later.

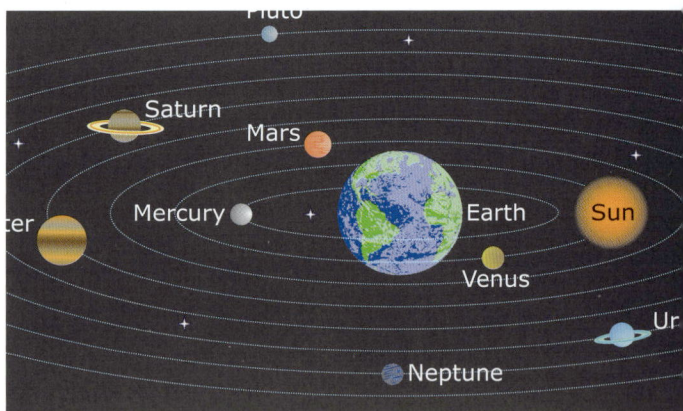

An ancient astronomer's view of our solar system. Can you spot the Sun?

Things to do

Discoveries

Ideas about our solar system and how it works have changed over many centuries. Many people have added to the ideas. Not all of them were right. But some of them were very clever.

- Find out what order the first astronomers put the planets in. You will need to use the Internet to do this.
- Make a timeline of all the changes and discoveries.

Galileo Galilei is said to have invented the telescope. This isn't true. He did however design bigger and better ones to look at the stars and the Sun.

- Use different magnifying lenses to make your own telescope. You may also need some black card. Why?
- What shape of lenses works best? Do not look directly at the Sun.

A telescope uses two or more lenses to magnify things

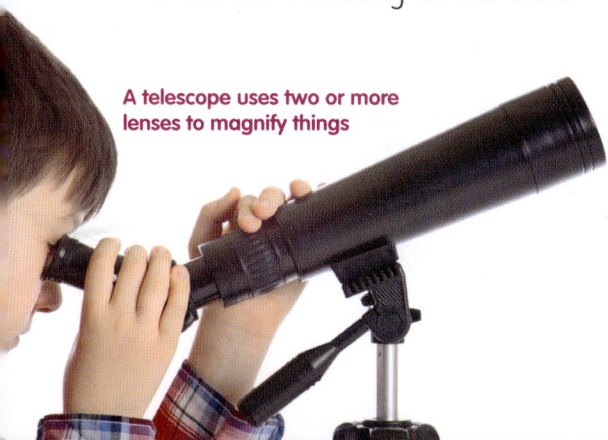

I wonder...

Are there still more planets to discover in our solar system?

Dig deeper

Find out:

- Claudius Ptolemy, another Greek philosopher, agreed with Aristotle that the Earth was at the centre of the universe. In what order did he place the planets, the Sun and Moon in his model of the universe?
- What did the astronomer Alhazen say about Ptolemy's research?
- What was the first law that Johannes Kepler made about the motion of the planets?

Did you know?

- Isaac Newton first explained gravity. He said that all objects had the power to pull things towards them. The Sun is very big and pulls things towards it.
- The Earth's gravity holds the moon in the sky.
- There are still people today who believe that the Earth is flat!

Night and day

Things to learn

- What causes day and night and how long it takes.
- What direction the Sun rises and sets in.
- How sunrise and sunset times change during the year.

Day and night

The Earth spins anticlockwise (when viewed looking down on the North Pole) on its axis once every 24 hours. This is why we get day and night. As the Earth rotates, we move into the Sun's light and call it 'day'. As the Earth goes on rotating, we move out of the Sun's light into darkness, which we call 'night'.

This photo shows that part of the Earth is lit by the Sun while the other part is in darkness. As the Earth spins around, the part in darkness moves into the light.

Half the Earth is always in shadow

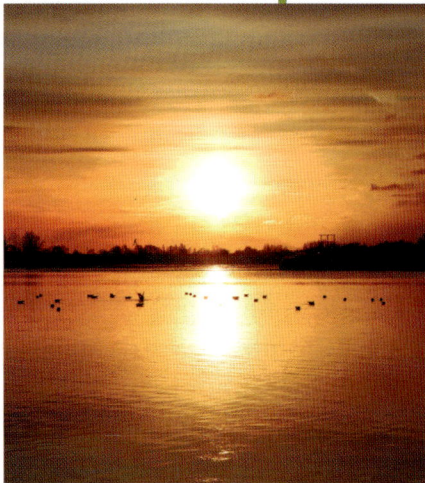

Sunrise, sunset

When the Sun comes over the horizon in the morning we call it **sunrise**. When the Sun disappears behind the horizon at dusk we call it **sunset**.

Your part of the world comes into daylight in the early morning. You will begin to see the Sun rise in the east. By midday you'll be directly facing the Sun. It will be in its highest position. At dusk, your part of the Earth will be moving into darkness. You will see the Sun set towards the west. The Sun is not actually moving across the sky. The Earth is spinning in front of it!

You will need to be on a west coast to see the sun set over the sea

Things to do

Daylight diary

- Find the sunrise and sunset times for each month from a newspaper or the Internet. Work out the day length. Plot your results on a graph. What pattern do you notice?

Day and night on other planets

All the planets in our solar system rotate. They all have day and night. However, they take different times to complete one spin.

- Find out the length of a day on other planets in our solar system. Which planet has a day that is longer than its year?

Jupiter takes 10 hours to spin on its axis once

Dig deeper

Find out:
- more about the length of day and night in different parts of the Earth.

If I lived on Jupiter, and I slept for eight hours a night, I'd only have two hours left in the day to eat and go to school!

Did you know?

- The ancient Babylonians divided the day into 12 parts instead of 24 hours.
- In summer at the North Pole it is always light because the Sun never sets.

I wonder…

Why is there more daylight in summer than in winter?

The Moon

Things to learn

- How long it takes the Moon to orbit the Earth.
- How the Moon appears to change as it orbits the Earth and the Earth spins.
- How we can see the Moon.

We see the Moon because the part facing the Sun reflects light into our eyes

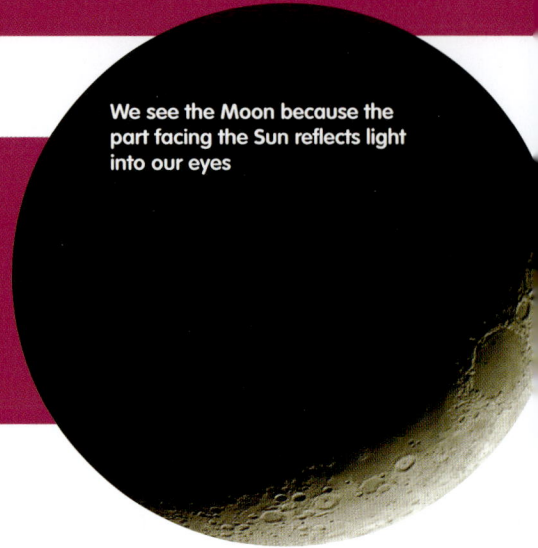

Moonshine

Although the Moon appears to be very bright it has no light of its own. It reflects light from the Sun. Sometimes the Moon is lit up by sunlight reflected from the Earth. This is called 'earthshine'.

The Moon's phases

As the Moon **orbits** the Earth, the light from the Sun shines on different parts of its surface. This makes the Moon appear to change shape. We call these changes the **phases** of the Moon.

The Moon's orbit

The Earth orbits the Sun, and the Moon orbits the Earth. Both the Earth and the Moon spin as they orbit. The Moon takes about 28 days to orbit the Earth. We call this a lunar month. The word 'month' comes from the word 'moon'.

Changing faces

When the side of the Moon facing us has no sunlight shining on it, we can't see it. We call this new Moon. The Sun is shining on the side of the Moon we can't see. We call it full Moon when the Sun lights all of the side facing the Earth.

The Moon takes the same time to spin on its axis as it does to orbit the Earth. This means that we only ever see one side of the Moon. As we see more of the surface lit up we say the Moon is **waxing**. The Moon is **waning** when the lit part starts to get smaller.

Model the Moon

Demonstrate how the Moon waxes and wanes.

- Paint a ball half black and half white – this represents your Moon, partly in shadow. Put a strong light at one side of the classroom to represent the Sun. Sit a friend on a chair in the centre of the room to represent the Earth.
- Holding the ball, orbit the Earth! Keep the white side of your model Moon facing the Sun at all times – that's the part that's lit up. Walk around the Earth. What does your friend see? As you orbit the Earth you should see the Moon go through all of its phases. Painting the ball black makes the shadow stronger – but there is no dark side to the Moon!

Moon diary

- Keep a diary of the shape of the Moon for a month. Each night, if you are able to see it, draw the shape of the Moon. Can you see the Moon going through its phases?

I wonder…

How does the movement of the Moon affect the tides on Earth?

Dig deeper

Find out:
- about the first man on the Moon, an American astronaut called Neil Armstrong.

Did you know?

- It takes astronauts three days to reach the Moon in a rocket.
- The first people to see the far side of the Moon were the crew of Apollo 8 when they circled the Moon in 1968.
- The footprints left by astronauts who stood on the Moon are still there because there is no wind, rain or weather to disturb them.

The passing year

Things to learn

- What one complete orbit of the Sun by a planet is called.
- How long the Earth takes to orbit the Sun.

Happy birthday

An astronomical year is how long it takes a planet to travel around or orbit the Sun once. The path the Earth takes around the Sun is called its orbit. It is not a circle but a slightly oval shape called an ellipse. The Earth takes 365¼ days to orbit the Sun. We call this a year.

A year on another planet is a different length from a year on Earth. Use the information in the table to work out how old you would be on other planets.

Leap years

You can't really have 365¼ days in a year. So every four years, we have a leap year with 366 days. This extra day, 29 February, is made up of the extra quarter day in each of the four years. If we didn't have the extra day, your birthday would creep forward through your life. You might start with a summer birthday and end up with a winter one! If you can divide the number of the year by four, that means it's a leap year. For instance, 1996, 2000, 2004, and 2008 are leap years. How many birthdays would you have had if you had been born on 29 February?

Planet	Time in Earth days to orbit the Sun
Mercury	88 days
Venus	225 days
Mars	688 days

The seasons

Another way of measuring the year is by the passing of the seasons.

Seasons are marked by changes in temperature and day length. Europe and Australia have four seasons: spring, summer, autumn and winter. Some places near the equator have two seasons: the rainy and the dry season. The Hindu calendar has six seasons.

How many seasons does your country have?

Why are some seasons hotter than others?

As the Moon orbits the Earth it spins. As the Earth orbits the Sun it spins

Things to do

How the Earth travels

Model how the Earth is travelling in space around the Sun. You will need to label the Sun, the Earth and the Moon, and have a big space to work in. Ask someone to explain what is going on, and present your 'play' to the rest of the class or school.

Make a calendar

A calendar is a record of the year.

- Design a calendar page for each month of the year. You could use a computer program to help you. Think about the changing seasons and the events and festivals that mark each month.

Dig deeper

Find out:
- how the changes in the seasons throughout the year affect animals.

Did you know?

- Before the modern calendar, Muslims had to put in an extra month to keep the seasons in the right place.
- Arctic ground squirrels hibernate for nine months of the year.
- The coldest place where people live all through the year is the village of Oymyakon in Russia, where the temperature can be 70°C below freezing in winter.

What have you learned? ✔

- The Sun, Earth and Moon are all spherical.
- The Sun is a star at the centre of our solar system.
- It takes 365¼ days for the Earth to orbit the Sun. This is one year.
- The Earth spins on its axis once every 24 hours. This is one day.
- At any one time part of the Earth is in darkness (night) and part in sunlight (day).
- Sunrise and sunset times change during the year.
- The Moon orbits the Earth once every 28 days.
- The Moon shines with reflected light from the Sun.
- The shape of the Moon changes throughout every 28 days. These are called its phases.
- Many scientists have contributed to how we understand the solar system.

Find out more about…

- if we are alone in the universe. Some people claim to have seen alien spacecraft and even to have met creatures from other star systems!
- the different ways people have made calendars using the Sun, Moon and stars.

Check-up

- Why do we sometimes get an eclipse of the Sun? Why are they quite rare?
- Why isn't the Moon between us and the Sun all the time? Is the Moon big enough to cover the Sun? Why doesn't the Moon shine through a **solar eclipse**? Think about what you know about sizes and distances.

The answer!

Do you remember the question about the disappearing star? This is because the Earth is spinning. As the Earth rotates it looks as if the entire sky is moving. Stars that are high in the sky early in the evening will become lower later on. Some may be hidden by buildings or walls.

What do you know?

- Think about these statements.
- Which do you know? Which have you learned?

- I have learned to describe a living organism.
- I have learned to talk about what I observe.
- I know that all living organisms grow and reproduce.
- I know what a microbe needs to grow.
- I have learned to make and record regular observations of bread mould.
- I can explain why dry, cold bread didn't grow mould.
- I know that we can't live without microbes.
- I have learned to plot a bar chart of my results.
- I know to change only one factor when investigating making bread.

What do you know?
- Think about these statements.
- Which do you know? Which have you learned?

- I have learned to identify parts of my body.
- I have learned to observe my body when I exercise.
- I know that animals need food to survive.
- I have learned to make observations of a person at rest and a person exercising.
- I know that without a proper diet I will become ill.
- I have learned to time the amount of exercise I take.
- I have learned where my heart is and I can find my pulse.
- I have learned to plot data into a bar chart and explain what it means.
- I know that my heart pumps blood around my body and why my muscles need oxygen.
- I have learned to plot my data into a line graph and say what happens to my heart when I exercise.

What do you know?
- Think about these statements.
- Which do you know? Which have you learned?

- I have learned to describe a living organism.
- I have learned to name some animals.
- I can talk about what I observe.
- I can talk about the conditions that animals and plants need to survive.
- I can talk about what plants need sunlight for.
- I know that all living organisms grow and reproduce.
- I have learned to make and record regular observations of my seeds.
- I have learned how pollen and seeds are dispersed.
- I have learned why insects are important to pollination.
- I have learned why my seeds without water didn't germinate.
- I have learned what seeds do need to germinate.
- I have learned the parts of a flower.
- I have learned why the seeds in the dark germinated as well as the ones in the light.
- I have learned to plot a bar chart of my results.
- I have learned what each part of a flower is for.
- I know why a flower needs to be pollinated.
- I have learned the stages of a human life cycle and a plant life cycle.
- I have learned that repeating an investigation or using lots of seeds gets better results.

What do you know?

- Think about these statements.
- Which do you know? Which have you learned?

- I have learned to describe my investigations of light correctly.
- I have learned to record my discoveries accurately.
- I know how to change the size and shape of shadows.
- I have learned to make and record my own observations.
- I have learned similarities and differences between light sources, lights and shadows.
- I have learned to compare and describe the brightness of lights and the depths of shadows.
- I have my own ideas about finding things out.
- I know that I record what I see so I can make comparisons.
- I have learned to measure distances accurately.
- I know how to keep an investigation fair.
- I have learned to see the patterns in my results, and give reasons for them.
- I have learned how I might have done an investigation better.
- I have learned to link shadow size with distance from a screen, or shadow length with the apparent movement of the Sun.
- I have learned to measure the amount of light.
- I have learned to make statements like 'The lower the Sun, the longer the shadow.'
- I have learned to make up my own fair test for light or shadows.
- I can explain how we see.
- I can say what I think will happen.
- I know what equipment I will need and how to use it.
- I have learned to record my results in a table and transfer them to a bar chart.
- I have learned to record my results on a line graph and tell its story.
- I can explain what I have found out, and how I could do it better.
- I can describe how light is reflected from a mirror.
- I know why it is important to record discoveries.
- I can make statements like 'Shiny surfaces reflect light better than dull surfaces.'

Unit 5: Changing state checklist

What do you know?
- Think about these statements.
- Which do you know? Which have you learned?

- I have learned to give examples of evaporation and condensation.
- I can explain what happens when materials evaporate and condense.
- I have learned to use a thermometer accurately.
- I can explain why evaporation and condensation are reversible.
- I can describe the rain or water cycle.
- I have learned to measure the volume of a liquid.
- I can explain how water can be purified by evaporation and condensation.
- I have learned to use the words evaporation and condensation accurately.
- I have learned to plan and complete a fair test with help.
- I can say how changing conditions affect evaporation and condensation.
- I have learned to plan and complete a fair test without help.

Unit 6: The Earth and beyond checklist

What do you know?
- Think about these statements.
- Which do you know? Which have you learned?

- I have learned to talk about the relative movements of the Earth and Moon around the Sun.
- I know that the Sun is a source of light, and that the Moon reflects its light.
- I have learned the relative movements of the Earth and Moon around the Sun.
- I have learned to define a day, a year and a month.
- I know that the rotation of the Earth results in day and night.
- I can define seasonal changes.
- I have learned to make observations of the apparent movement of the Sun.
- I have learned to record how the Sun appears to move across the sky and how the Moon appears to change shape.
- I can describe annual changes in day length.
- I have learned to measure, record and display daily changes in shadow length.
- I have learned to keep records of change like the phases of the Moon.
- I have learned the apparent movement of the Sun.
- I can describe seasonal change.
- I can describe the apparent change in the Moon's shape.
- I have learned to record changes like day length as a graph.
- I have learned to model and explain changes caused by the movement of the Earth and Moon.
- I can explain the apparent movement of the Sun.
- I can explain the cause of seasonal change.
- I can explain the apparent change in the Moon's shape.
- I have learned to make predictions about the Sun's apparent path and the Moon's apparent change in shape based on my knowledge.
- I can name some scientists who made discoveries about the solar system.

Glossary

addictive – something that is difficult to stop using, taking or doing

anther – part of a flower that makes pollen

artery – thick-walled blood vessel, carries blood away from the heart

astronomer – person who studies space

axis – an imaginary line that something spins around

bacteria – single-celled microbes

balanced diet – healthy mixture of foods that meet all your needs

beam – a ray of light

binocular vision – seeing with two eyes

biotechnology – using living organisms to make food, medicines and other products

block – to stand in the way of or stop

boiling point – the temperature atwhich something boils. For water this is 100°C

capillary – fine blood vessel

carbohydrates – energy-producing foods, such as starch, sugar and glucose

carpel – female part of a flower

compost – plant material rotted by bacteria, used as a fertilizer

condense – to change from gas to liquid

curing – preserving food by salting, drying or smoking

disperse – to scatter or spread

drug – something that causes a change in our bodies, good or bad

evaporate – to change from liquid to gas

extinct – no longer in existence

fertilization – when male and female elements combine to make new life

filament – the stalk of the male anther of a flower

flammable – something that can burn easily

freeze – to change from liquid to solid

germ – a harmful microbe or micro-organism that causes disease

germinate – to sprout or bud; the first growth of a seed

gestation – the time a mammal baby is in its mother; pregnancy

irradiating – a way to preserve food that kills microbes by giving the food a dose of radiation

life cycle – full circle of a plant or animal life

light – source that makes things visible, such as the Sun, an electric light or a lit candle

light sensitive – responds to the level of light it is subjected to

medicine – a type of drug used to help us recover or get better

melt – to change state from solid to liquid

micro-organisms – living things usually too small to be seen by the naked eye (microbes)

Moon – Earth's natural satellite

offspring – the young of an animal or plant

opaque – materials that don't let light through

orbit – to circle round

ovum – part of a flower where seeds form

pasteurize – to heat a liquid to a high temperature to kill bacteria

petal – coloured part of a flower

phase – state or period, such as a phase of the Moon

planet – large round object that orbits a star

pollen – dust that contains the male element of a flowering plant

pollinate – to transfer pollen from the anther to the stamen of a flower

preserved – kept unchanged

pulse – pressure wave of the heartbeat through the body

pupate – when an insect changes from a larva to a pupa

reflection – when light bounces from a shiny object into our eyes

reproducte – to produce offspring

satellite – an object that orbits a planet

scattered – thrown in different directions

shadow – dark shape that falls on a surface when the path of light is blocked

silhouette – picture or portrait made by cutting out the shape of a shadow from black paper

solar eclipse – where the Moon passes between the Earth and the Sun so you can't see the Sun for a time

solidify – to change from liquid to solid

source – the place something starts from, e.g. a torch is a source of light

space – outer space, the place where stars and planets are found

sphere – globe, ball

spin – to turn on an axis

stamen – male part of a flower

starch – carbohydrate food found in cereals and potatoes

sterilize – make clean or free from bacteria

stigma – pollen lands on this part of a flower

style – holds the stigma of a flower

sugar – carbohydrate food found in many foods used to make food and drinks taste sweet

sunrise – when the Sun rises in the eastern sky

sunset – when the Sun sets in the western sky

translucent – materials that let some light through

transparent – material that is see-through

travel – moves

vein – a thin-walled blood vessel, carries blood to the heart

vessel – a blood vessel is a tube

waning – getting smaller

water cycle – closed path of water from rain through cloud and back to the sea again

waxing – getting larger

Index